CO ANTRIM

Edited by Dave Thomas

First published in Great Britain in 1999 by
YOUNG WRITERS
Remus House,
Coltsfoot Drive,
Woodston,
Peterborough, PE2 9JX
Telephone (01733) 890066

All Rights Reserved

Copyright Contributors 1999

HB ISBN 0 75431 590 8
SB ISBN 0 75431 591 6

FOREWORD

Young Writers have produced poetry books in conjunction with schools for over eight years; providing a platform for talented young people to shine. This year, the Celebration 2000 collection of regional anthologies were developed with the millennium in mind.

With the nation taking stock of how far we have come, and reflecting on what we want to achieve in the future, our anthologies give a vivid insight into the thoughts and experiences of the younger generation.

We were once again impressed with the quality and attention to detail of every entry received and hope you will enjoy the poems we have decided to feature in *Celebration 2000 Co Antrim* for many years to come.

CONTENTS

Ashgrove Primary School

Brian Falloon	1
Kyle Graham	1
Tania Reid	2
Emma McWhirter	2
Sheryl McBride	3
Brooke Scott	4
David Moore	4
Jack Courtney	5
Ruth Carson	6
Rebekah Startin	7
Stephen West	7
Hayley Campbell	8
Michaela Crowe	8
Stacey Harrison	9
Steven Calvert	9
Kristine Donnan	10
David Cinnamond	10
Kelly Sproule	11
Mathew Anderson	12
Kirsty Lowry	13
Darren Craig	14
Naomi Campbell	14
Danielle Scanlon	15
Helen Armstrong	16
Jonathan Seeds	16
Francis Pattison	17
Mark Reid	17
Katrina Meek	18
Donna McFerran	18
Rebecca Trew	19
Sarah Tilbury	19
Kyle Peoples	19
Stacie Novotny	20
Aisha Anwar	20
Aaron McClean	21

Lucy Davis	21
Leah McFall	22
Jonathan Harper	22
Carole King	23
Hayley Smyth	23
Danielle Fletcher	24
Joshua Chisim	24
Ashleigh Dornan	25
Lynsay Morrison	25
Stacey Keel	26
Christopher Mehaffey	26
Neil Whiteside	27
Laura Thompson	27
Abigail Ramsay	28
Ryan Montgomery	28
Johnathan Chivers	29
Charys Anderson	29
Holly Cochrane	29
Cheryl Keel	30
Rayhaanah Ali	30
Carly Young	31
Jonathan Boyd	31
Margaret Watt	32
Natasha Tumilson	32
Linzi Ferguson	32
Debra Bell	33
Joanne Lockhart	33
Matthew Boyd	33
Rebecca Hamilton	34
Heather Davidson	34
Shauna McCann	35
Kirsty McNutt	35
Sarah Davidson	36
Rebecca Ingram	36
Lauren Collins	37
Hannah Carmichael	37

Ballymacash Primary School

Suzi Bradley	37
Julie Stewart	38
Christopher Richmond	38
Richard Hanna	39
Christopher Morrow	39
Angela Champion	40
Deborah McCarthy	40
Hannah Kelly	41
Gary Keep	41
Arlene Robinson	41
Sharon Magee	42
Matthew McCarthy	42
Cheryl McClean	42
Ashlene Dalzell	43
Kassandera Patton	43
Jason Haydon	44
Ryan Lynn	44
Lisa McLaren	44
Hayley Topping	45
Rachael McCord	45
Michaela Robinson	45
Arran Crossey	46

Ballymacward Primary School

Joanna Cushnahan	46
Carla Mulholland	48
Ashleen Mulholland	48
Clara McStravick	49
Kevin Higgins	49
Mark Lynch	50
Fiona Hagan	50
Jonathan Jones	51
Bernadette Goan	51

Broughshane Primary School

Lynne McCosh	52
Lee Murphy	52

Kristi Robinson	53
Mark Foster	54
Joe Adams	54
Megan Lennox	55
Gordon Davidson	56
Ian Mark	56
Joanne Currie	57
Dean Campbell	58
Jason Clyde	58
Ruarcc McAloon	59
Aaron Bailie	59
Andrea McNeill	60
Richard Allen	60
Howard Jamieson	61
Jennifer Millar	62
Richard Montford	62
Lisa Douglas	63
Peter Kennedy	64
Lisa-Jane Millar	64
Sarah Kernohan	65
Dar Óma McAloon	66
Suzanne Smyth	66
Loise Boyd	67
Gemma McClenaghan	68
Philip McBurney	68
Stuart Kennedy	69
Tanya Wilson	69
Mark Loughridge	70
Jane Burgess	70
Patricia Boyd	71
Aaron Doyle	71
Keri Smyth	72
Christina Fleck	72
Nigel Elliott	73
Mark McNeill	74

Buick Memorial Primary School

Gemma Eaton	74

James Matthew Fenton	75
Elaine Campbell	76
Ashley McIlroy	77

Cloughmills Primary School

Andrew Linton	78
Alex Hunter	78
Adrian Boyd	79
David Adams	79
Holly Matthews	80
Ashley Kirker	80
Naomie Campbell	80
Natasha Linton	81
Stacey McFetridge	81
Lee Shannon	82
Susie Houston	82
Lyndsey Rock	83
Leanne Strange	83
Laura Millar	84
Colin Givens	84
Michaela McKnight	85
Rebecca Sweetlove	85
Pauline McDonald	85

Harmony Hill Primary School

Rachel Hanna	86
Alice Moffitt	86
Victoria Irving	87
Timothy Atkinson	87
Kirsty McAuley	88
Charlotte Matless	88
David Henry	89
Alastair Toner	89
Keith Hannigan	90
Anthony Rough	90
Naomi Foster	91
Sarah Mawhinney	91
Andrew Stewart	92

Aaron Coulter	93
Leighanne Wright	94
David Harkness	95
Emma Gill	95
Ashleigh McCoosh	96
Lynsey Jess	97
Nicola Henry	97
Rebecca McCrossan	98
Melissa Harris	98
Jenny Doherty	99
Ruth Thompson	100
Craig Loney	100
Alan Whitten	101
Lauren Megaw	102
Ross Helsdon	102
Amy Porter	103
Scott Matthews	103
Lycette Harris	104
Laura Rodgers	105
Patrick Stevenson	105
Nicola McGarel	106
Jason Kerr	106
Sarah Howes	107
Shona Baldwin	108
Mark Gribben	109
Michael Hunter	109
Christopher Brady	110

Killowen Primary School

Christopher Boyd	110
Craig Hendley	111
Nicole Hill	111
Natasha Wilson	112
David Atchison	112
Christopher Cowgill	113
Daniel Agahi	113
Gary McCreery	114
Gillian Martin	114

Lauren Wilson	115
Dean McFall	116
Grace Morrison	116
Ryan Garvin	117

Knockmore Primary School

Chantelle Phillips	117
Laura Moag	118
Claire Armstrong	118
Leigh Pauley	119
David Flanagan	120

Moorfields Primary School

Emma White	120
Gayle Armstrong	121
Brian Houston	121
Alison Marks	122
Daena Carrie Lipsett	122
Frew Johnston	123
Pamela Livingstone	124
Deborah Storey	124
Selina Shingleton	125

Mossley Primary School

James Spence	126
Darryl McConnell	126
Michael Mahon	126
Jonathan Acheson	127
Sarah Lynas	127
Gary Johnston	127
Dale Huston	128
Matthew Boyd	128
Andrew Innes	128
Sarah Knight	129
Matthew McCracken	129
Graeme Adam Fitzsimmons	130
Karl Cosgrove	130
Daniel Watson	131

Gary Couser	131
Rebecca Davidson	132
Mark Fenning	132
Benjamin Thomas Davis	133
Matthew Wilson	133
Victoria Braden	134
Adam Anderson	134
Jonathan Lowans	134
Steven Davidson	135
Lesley Ann Hoey	135
Fiona Young	136
Darren Taylor	136
Hyunchul Yang	137
Danielle Earley	137
Stephen Monaghan	137
Simon McMullan	138
Noel Beckett	138
Phillip Sloan	139
Andrew Nicholl	139
Cassie Clair Arkins	139
Amy Cooke	140
Claudia Ashe	140
Rebekah Fenning	141
Daniel Barnett	141
Rebecca Edgar	142

Oakfield Primary School

Clare Wallace	142
Brian Irvine	143
Claire Crawford	143
Claire Auld	144
Rhonda Humphreys	144
Susan Jones	145
Christopher Johnston	146

Parkgate Primary School

Richard McMillan	146
Ryan Irvine	147

Simon McClay	147
Daniel McMillan	148
Adam McClay	148
Lisa McCartney	149
Kelly Ann Connor	149
Sarah Cuthbertson	150
Natasha Henderson	150
Jamie McMillan	151

Rathenraw Integrated Primary School

Louise Adair	151
Michael Knox	152
Christopher McClelland	152
Sarah El-Hamalawy	153
Martina Reed	153
David McClelland	154
Robert Smith	154
Mairead Gribbon	154
Victoria Patty	155
Steven Jones	155
Graeme Clarke	155
John Mulholland	156

St Catherine's Primary School, Belfast

Natalie Smyth	156
Sadhbh Smyth	157
Deirdre Bowman	157
Margaret Sarah Mooney	158
Roisin Flynn	158
Caron Donnelly	159
Lisa Cosgrove	159
Isabelle McHenry	160

St Colman's Primary School, Lambeg

Siobhan Crummey	160
Ciaron Flannery	161
Deborah Kearney	161
Brendan Wright	162

Kathryn McCann	162
Claire Kennedy	163
Seanin Sands	164
James Ferguson	164
Tara Watterson	165
Bridgeen Conlon	165
Cormac McCloskey	166
Carl Adams	166
Conor O'Reilly	167
Conall Mulhern	167
Alice Hamill	168
Aaron Feeney	168
Melissa Marlow	169
Maeve Power	169
Emer O'Kane	170
Katie Stanley	170
Dillon McDonnell	171
Aidan Kelly	171
Kerry Watterson	172
Roisin Maguire	172
Orlaith Moran	173
Meabh Trainor	173
Emma McCrory	174
Lauren Bailie	175
Conor Maguire	176

St Patrick's Primary School, Portrush

Jamie Cassidy	177
Conard McCullagh	177
Cal Hunter	178
Sorcha Loughrey	178
Joanne Quinn	179
Kieran McNicholl	180
Ciara Etherson	180
Fergus McFaul	181
David Donaghy	182
Roisin Donnelly	182
Meghan Doole	183

Dean Murphy	184
Adrian McCullagh	184
Owen McLaughlin	185
Lauren Doherty	186
Amy Lagan	187
Gemma Hegarty	188
Claire McNally	188
Niamh Quinn	189
Martin McAlister	190
Mary McCrory	190

Springfarm Primary School

Laura Cunningham	191

Straid Primary School

Martin Davey	191
Edmund Davis	192
Christopher Walker	192
Jane McAllister	193
Ariane Moore	194
Craig Bunting	194
Joel Dundee	195
Sarah Harrison	195
James Hutchinson	196
Hannah Buckley	196
Glenn Irwin	197
Louise Forsythe	198
Lauren Glasgow	198
Samuel Forsythe	199

The Poems

MY BABY DRAGON SMOKEY

I have a baby dragon, his name is Smokey
Sometimes I bring him to school with me
Sometimes I don't
Of course he can't breathe fire yet
But he will soon
When I put him in my school bag he says
'Hey! Get me out of here.'
Sometimes he reads my library books
That's how he learns to read
And he nibbles my homework book
That's how I get shouted at by Mr Morrow
When I looked in my bag
All I could see was paper everywhere
And when Mr Morrow asked me for my homework
I didn't know what to say
But apart from that
I love my baby dragon Smokey.

Brian Falloon (10)
Ashgrove Primary School

SUMMER

Summer is sunny
Young children playing with their bunnies
Mums sunbathing in the sun
Mums getting up to make the dinner
Eating ice-lollies
Remember the sunny weather
Now it's winter.

Kyle Graham (8)
Ashgrove Primary School

MY DOG

My dog Tara has black and brown fur,
She licks me on my hand,
A special part to her.

She eats a lot of montonas,
Which have in them a lot of sultanas,
She likes it very much.

She plays with the toys,
Which make lots of noise
And she chases away the boys.

When Tara goes to bed
She takes her teddy bear, Ted,
She likes Ted very much.

Now she has a family,
5 girls, 2 boys and a husband.
That's my dog Tara.

Tania Reid (10)
Ashgrove Primary School

WHY I LIKE ANIMALS

Horses like to gallop in the fields,
and hamsters go round and round
in their wheels.
Puppies are loyal, faithful and true
but are always trying to bite your shoe,
while rabbits are fluffy and
cuddly and nice,
and sleek, little cats get rid of mice.

Emma McWhirter (9)
Ashgrove Primary School

MY HORSE

As I walk away from my horse
I go and get in my mum's flashy Porsche
I'm going to my riding school
To see my riding instructor's mule.

I'm bringing my horse to a show
I'm going to win this I know
My partner is called Hannah
Her pony is called Susanah.

Oh look we've won first place
Kerry will have to start packing her case
For now we are at the top
Nobody is going to make us stop.

My horse is tired and so am I
Now I am looking to the sky
In my tent I feel like John Wayne
Oh no it's starting to rain.

Up again I'm soaked to the skin
My riding kit was thrown in the bin
All the red dye was smudged into my jods'
Since we're out in the car let's go to Mauds.

At Mauds we got strawberry ice-creams
My mum got a video called 'How to Cook with Beans'
I brought my horse to Barley Cove Bay
For him to run about and play.

But now the day is away
My horse cannot play
And now I will go away to bed
To rest my very sleepy head.

Sheryl McBride (10)
Ashgrove Primary School

THE CITY AT NIGHT

Lovely sun is shining bright
Behind the moon.
Beautiful gleaming stars.
Some people having
A feast in their lovely cosy houses.
Children in their rooms
Tucked up in bed
Having lovely dreams.
Curtains all pulled over like
Eyelids, closed.
Wind blowing in the trees.
Waste bin lid banging up and down.
Branches crackling and leaves blowing around.
The sun is rising up and up.
Now it is morning,
Time for school,
Get your bags and hurry up
Or you'll be late.
Goodbye Mummy, have a good day.
Oh no look at the traffic,
There are a lot of pretty cars.
I think it is better at night
Because it is not so busy.

Brooke Scott (8)
Ashgrove Primary School

MY DOG

My dog is a puppy
She eats puppy food
She likes to chew dog bones
Her name is Connie
She likes to play with me
I bought her a ball for Christmas and a bone.

When I go out to play she cries for me and Jamie
She jumps up on the door trying to open it
She chews everything especially me and Jamie.

David Moore (9)
Ashgrove Primary School

CHOOSING A BOOK

Choosing a book I have to discover
Should I pick it by the looks of the cover?
My dad said get one about kings
So I go to the library on the next fine day.
I look at a book that makes me say
'Why do they make books based on art?'
So then I walk up lane five
The books there were about being alive.
I walked away from the science books,
Soon I had a look and then I found it.
It was called 'Choosing A Book.'
So I borrowed the book and travelled home,
I sat on my bed and fiddled with my comb.
I remembered my book that I had borrowed,
I started to read it. It began with Rome,
It gave me a clue
So I tied my shoe
And went to the library
And shouted 'Yahoo!'
Now I am good at picking books
So I just have to take a few looks
And there it is. A very good story.
It worked like a charm; a piece of glory.

Jack Courtney (10)
Ashgrove Primary School

THE CHICKEN

Poor old chicken's gonna be dead
Sly Mr Foxy's dreaming in his bed
Thinking about how little chickens gettin' killed
The sly Fox family will have a fatter build.

Little Miss Chicken roosting in her nest
Thinking of eggs and which are the best.
The fox is on his way to the farm
He's got his very best lucky charm.

Ma Fox is laying the table
Baby Fox wants to; she says he's not able.
Mr Fox is sneaking past the barn
Baby Fox is dreaming he'd be home from the farm.

Sly Mr Fox is outside the hen house
Being as quiet as a little mouse.
Little Miss Chick does not have a clue
This rubbish about foxes is all very new.

Oh no! Mr Fox has pounced on her now
The little hen's fighting back! How?
She's pecking and squawking and flapping about
She's pecking his eyes and punching him out.

She's gathering up all her friends right now
And forcing the fox to tell her how
To get to the den where the mother stays
So they can beat them up in all different ways.

Poor Fox family lying dead
Little Miss Chicken dreaming happily in bed
Of visions of sugar plums in her head.
No wonder she's happy! The foxes are dead.

Ruth Carson (10)
Ashgrove Primary School

AUTUMN

Autumn is my favourite season
I like it a lot because it's very pleasing.
Autumn is also very colourful
With all those beautiful leaves
Of red and yellow, orange and brown
Falling, falling, from the trees.
In autumn it is my birthday,
In '99 I'll be eleven.
My cousin will have her birthday party too
But she will only be seven.
Autumn is full of lovely smells
From the twigs and crunchy leaves
And when I'm in the forest
With that I cannot disagree.
The weather in autumn is cold
And the days they do get shorter.
But don't go in, just stay outside
Until Mum calls you in for supper.

Rebekah Startin (10)
Ashgrove Primary School

TEACHERS

Teachers give you far too much homework.
Teachers give you too much work.
Teachers are very boring.
Teachers sit on their bums all day.
Teachers keep you back after the bell goes.
Teachers are all grumpy as goats.
Teachers, who do they think they are?
Teachers shout 'be quiet', when we are already quiet.

Stephen West (10)
Ashgrove Primary School

TEACHERS

Teachers, who do they think they are?
They sit all day on their lazy bums
Making us do lots and lots of work.
They shout, 'Be quiet, be quiet!'
Do they ever give over?
They keep us back after the bell goes and never let us go,
They're far too grumpy that's probably why.

Teachers give us far too much homework
And expect us to have it done for the next day.
Teachers are extremely bossy and never give over,
They just laze about; rabbitting about:
Well I don't think you would really want to know,
I'm sure you wouldn't.

Hayley Campbell (10)
Ashgrove Primary School

ON A WINTER'S NIGHT

The nights of winter are frozen and white,
The roofs are like blocks of ice
As stiff as anything.
The people are walking through the winter cold
To get to the shops.
The fire is on in every house,
The children are tucked up in bed with hot water bottles.
Every mum and dad have all got a cup of hot tea
To keep them warm.
All you can hear are car engines brooming along
On a winter's night.

Michaela Crowe (8)
Ashgrove Primary School

Winter

Snow is falling down and down
To the white and slippery ground
Everyone is slipping round and round
People are laughing at others falling down.

Winter is my favourite season
Because of all the snow on the hills
Children can laugh and play on their sleighs
But when they go in they are very cold.

Children love the season winter
Especially the month December
They love the 24th remember
Because Santa comes all night round.

Then we saw a bit of sun
And everybody said we might have no more fun
Then everybody was very sad
They went inside and played some more.

Stacey Harrison (10)
Ashgrove Primary School

Colours

Blue is the colour of the sky that sits on everything
Silver and gold the colour of the sharp, thick sword
Yellow is for the sun that shines in summer
Red is for the posters that sit on your wall
Green is for the bright grass that's in your back yard
Brown is for the dark bricks that build up your house
Grey is the air that flows all around you
White is for the borders that go around your wall

Steven Calvert (9)
Ashgrove Primary School

BROTHERS

Brothers, brothers, they are so annoying,
Always barging into your room; never ever knocking.
Oh those nasty horrible troublemakers!
My brother is so bad I think I'll have to sell him. Any takers?

Wrecking your room, breaking your toys
Those horrible brothers; bad, bad boys.
I really don't see why brothers have to exist
Punching, kicking and using their fist.

If you have a sister you're so lucky
Instead of a brother getting messy and mucky.
Sisters are kind; sisters are gentle
Whereas brothers are crazy, stupid and mental.

When I'm happily doing something quiet
My brother and his pal come in making a riot.
When my brother's got a sore tummy I'd advise you to put earmuffs on
For all through the house you can hear my brother shouting, 'Mummy!'

Oh brothers, brothers I wish they never lived
But when he was a baby he was cute with his bib.
But now he's all grown-up, punching and giving you a blister,
Oh really I wish I had a sister.

Kristine Donnan (10)
Ashgrove Primary School

HEALTH

If you smoke, *stop now!* It is silly.
All it does is blacken your lungs.
Never drink, it too can *kill!*

Always eat a balanced diet,
Don't eat a lot of sweets and buns,
Try to eat more fruit and vegetables.

Never drink too much Coke,
Drink more water and milk
Because they're much healthier and not so sweet.

Exercise more to keep your muscles and bones
Very strong and healthy.
Eat good food to encourage your cells to grow.

David Cinnamond (10)
Ashgrove Primary School

IN THE DEEP BLUE SEA

In the deep, blue sea
People go diving.
In the deep, blue sea
Fish swim about.
In the deep, blue sea
I can see two sea trout.

In the deep, blue sea
Crabs walk about.
In the deep, blue sea
Octopuses swim about.
In the deep, blue sea
Seahorses swim about.

In the deep, blue sea
Mermaids sit on stones.
In the deep, blue sea
Sharks have lots of fights.
In the deep, blue sea
Seaweed hangs about.

Kelly Sproule (9)
Ashgrove Primary School

SPORT

Sport is really such fun,
Especially when there's a big, yellow sun.
There's roads, there's pitches and there's more,
But at the end it depends on the score.

In rugby, men go dashing by
But when others tackle they nearly die.
They kick a ball through two big posts
Hoping they will get the most.

Motorsport, that's really mad.
Drivers, they are big and bad,
Around the corners really fast
Along the straight, they're zooming past.

There's swimming, running and there's darts,
There's sailing, snooker, men in carts.
Skiing, skating, tennis, racing
Horses, greyhounds, planes are chasing.

In football, people dribble the ball
Running rings that are big and small.
The silky passing, combinating
And when they score; the mad celebrating.

Running about, they are so crazy
Footballers are really not lazy.
Scissor kicks and blistering volleys
While all the fans are sucking lollies.

Owen, Shearer, Bergkamp too,
And all the stars their dreams came true.
Around the world everybody knows
Sports is the best and it really shows.

Mathew Anderson (10)
Ashgrove Primary School

TEACHERS

Teachers tell you to be quiet,
Then we all start a riot.
Teachers tell you to sit down,
Then we all dance around.

Teachers tell you what to do,
Teachers always shout at you,
Teachers tell you your work is wick,
Teachers tell you to be quick.

Teachers, who do they think they are?
Acting like a pretty flower,
Teachers shout all day.
Even when we are singing songs!

Teachers drinking cups of tea,
When we're all outside freezing.
Teachers chatting about all the work they're going to give us
While we're waiting for the buses.

Teachers munching at their lunch
While children eat up their brunch.
Teachers give you hard work to do,
Which is not very easy for you.

Teachers are planning work that's hard
While we are running in the yard.
Teachers do whatever they please,
Whilst we're doing work that's not a breeze.

Kirsty Lowry (10)
Ashgrove Primary School

In The House

PlayStation blaring, my sister scaring,
Mum singing, what a noise.
Dad ringing Fred in the big voice,
Someone ringing at the door.
Oh no, it's DC at the door!
Run for your lives!
DC comes in and throws
Me in the beehives.
When Mum calls for tea
We come and my sister and I
Have a race, fall and crash into a wall,
But of course, we all fall and she always cries,
But why, oh why does she have to cry?
Just why?
In the morning
My dad is moaning.
I am boring,
My sister is annoying
And I just hate Monday mornings!

Darren Craig (10)
Ashgrove Primary School

Outside In The Snow

Oh how we shiver,
Oh how we shake,
Oh how our teeth chatter,
Oh how cold is one snowflake.

Oh how warm are the teachers inside,
Drinking a hot cup of cappuccino with extra flake,
Talking! Oh what chatterboxes!
They even say 'Isn't it cold today?'

Then at lunch time they make us hurry
To freeze again, it's such a worry,
Outside at minus five degrees,
They're inside eating sandwiches and cheese.

Naomi Campbell (10)
Ashgrove Primary School

MY INVISIBLE TEACHER

One day when we came into school,
our teacher was not there.
We walked around the classroom for ages,
then came a voice out of nowhere,
'Hooray, hooray!
It's worked at last!
My latest invention is completed!
Now I shall rule the whole world!
Come on you stupid children, be seated!'
A boy in our class tried to open the door
but indeed, it was surely locked.
'You miserable little maggot,' said that voice again,
and you can imagine that boy was shocked.
'And now you will all be turned into worms!' said that voice in a
                                    frightening way,
'And most of all, you will curl up and die today!'

There is only one moral to this story;
Don't go to school, no matter what!
Drive your government up the wall,
stay at home and be safely taught!

Danielle Scanlon (9)
Ashgrove Primary School

WINTER

Snow is falling to the ground
Children playing all around.
Everyone laughing, having fun
All you can see is a little bit of sun.

All day long I'll play and play
Laughing, singing, happy and gay,
But I will be so very sad
Right at the end of the day.

Now the snow is melting
I am very sad,
But hopefully it will snow again,
Then I'll be very glad.

I'm not worried any more,
I'll have some fun in the sun
And I'll play
And play all day.

Helen Armstrong (10)
Ashgrove Primary School

MONSTER TRUCKS

Monster trucks are big and high
up to the ceiling, up to the sky.
Monster trucks are very loud,
they go over ramps and get
watched by the crowd.
Monster trucks' tyres are heavy too.
If they were in a car park you
would be too!

Jonathan Seeds (8)
Ashgrove Primary School

SUMMER

Summer is my favourite season
School is over and I'm not teasing
Children running out of school.

Puppies barking, cats maiowing, children shouting, babies yelling,
Birds singing in the trees; sun is shining,
Children drinking Coca-Cola; only a slight breeze.

The sky is blue, there is not a cloud for the sun to fight,
Not a raindrop is in sight.
The days are longer, the nights shorter.

The summer's ending very fast,
The days are really flying past,
It's back to school on Monday! Oh no!

Francis Pattison (10)
Ashgrove Primary School

IN THE CITY

In the city there are lots of sounds,
Sounds like cars booming, roaring.
Motorbikes zooming, diggers digging,
Even when you are in the shops you
Can hear music blaring loudly.
Buses zooming round and round
But I can't even hear a sound.
Lorries roaring close to the ground,
Cars booming very loud.
It is a very lovely sound.

Mark Reid (10)
Ashgrove Primary School

WHY DO WE HAVE SUMMER?

Why do we have summer?
Is it because children can't work when it's hot?
Or because teachers need a break?
Or because travel agents would be out of their jobs?

Do we have summer because of other people?
Because they can't just have three seasons?
Or because the sun wants a season to itself?
The sun might want that, but it's not right, is it?

Well, I don't think any are right,
But we have summer because of fruit and vegetables
And other living things. Summer is happy, bright and full of fun,
Summer is the time for me!

Katrina Meek (10)
Ashgrove Primary School

WINTER

Winter time,
I just love
winter, snow
and frost as
white as could be.
The fire, as warm
and red, orange and
yellow. All people sitting
round the fire
and nanny knitting
jumpers to keep
them warm.

Donna McFerran (9)
Ashgrove Primary School

Dogs

I love dogs,
I like them a lot,
I hate their secret talk.
They're always barking,
chewing up logs,
chasing cats everywhere.

Rebecca Trew (10)
Ashgrove Primary School

Sweets

Sweets, sweets, everyone eats.
They are such treats,
When you see them, your heart beats.
Then you need to sit down on a seat,
They are so scrumptious you can't resist.

Sarah Tilbury (9)
Ashgrove Primary School

Aliens

We all think that aliens are not true,
yet seven were found in the depths of Peru.
They killed an old man,
then went to Japan,
and there they killed one hundred and two!

Kyle Peoples (8)
Ashgrove Primary School

SEASONS

In spring the trees begin to sprout their leaves,
the flowers begin to grow.
The winter has gone for now,
so has the snow.

In summer, the sun fills the sky,
the days are getting late,
people having barbecues
on an ice cool plate.

In autumn, the leaves turn red, yellow and brown,
badgers and foxes hibernate underground.
Birds build their nests high in the trees
the leaves fall off with the lightest breeze.

In winter the snow will come again,
so will the ice,
but everyone is warm inside
so nobody minds.

Stacie Novotny (9)
Ashgrove Primary School

THE SUN

The sun shines all day long to keep us happy.
The sun tans us brown.
The sun makes us lively, to make us scream and laugh.
The sun makes the washing dry to make women happy.
The sun is always there and shines on us.
The sun will come when it pleases.
The sun will make us scream with joy.

Aisha Anwar (9)
Ashgrove Primary School

To Be A Millionaire

It is about me being a millionaire.
What would I buy?
Have lots of girls running after me!
People wanting autographs,
Mostly getting lots of money
To get games for my PlayStation.
Stay in hotels for a year,
Have tea with the President of the United States of America.
Go to space in a rocket!
But I would not keep it all to myself,
I would give some to charity.
I would give one thousand or two to my sister,
How kind!
When I have spent all my money,
No girls would run after me!

Aaron McClean (9)
Ashgrove Primary School

My Dog And My Hamster

My dog always lets my hamster on her back.
They can both type and they can go on and surf the Net.
They both play, sing, eat, drink and dance together.
My dog sometimes barks my hamster to sleep.
My hamster is called Max and my dog is called Pup.

Their favourite movie is Mania,
their favourite food is chips.
Their favourite TV programme is CDTV.
On the 19th of April, I am going to zoom
both of them into the Internet because they want to.

Lucy Davis (9)
Ashgrove Primary School

How I Wish I Was My Dog

How I wish I was my dog,
Looking like a little log.
She doesn't have to go to school,
She even gets to chase a bull.
She rolls in muck
Or chases a duck,
Oh, how I wish I was my dog.

We live near a farm
With a very big barn
Where she could chase a cat,
Or even a rat.
Go under the table
When she is able.

But there are some things that you couldn't do.
If I was a dog it wouldn't do to
Ask if you can have a snack,
Show your tears after a whack.
There are lots of things you couldn't do,
Like talking to your owner too.

So I think I'll stay the way I am,
Being able to talk to my mam.

Leah McFall (9)
Ashgrove Primary School

Little Robin

Little robin in the snow,
how do you survive in the snow?
It is cold, it is dark,
but I am warm on my rug.

Come in, come in,
snuggle into me,
I'll keep you warm.
It's dangerous outside, but safe with me.

Jonathan Harper (11)
Ashgrove Primary School

THE MOON

The moon is shining bright
in the middle of the night.
The stars keep on twinkling
as my bed clothes keep on crinkling.
My best friend is dreaming of a dove
as I keep staring at the stars above,
and in the day when I look at the
star chart in my classroom,
I go back again.

Carole King (8)
Ashgrove Primary School

THE WIND

The wind is soft, the wind is slow,
it whistles and blows
in the air.
The wind is everywhere.
It blows the plants,
it blows our hair.
When you are sitting on your chair,
it is out there . . . somewhere.

Hayley Smyth (8)
Ashgrove Primary School

PEOPLE

People can be black,
people can be white,
people can be fat,
people can be slim,
people can wear hairbands,
people can wear rings,
people can have animals,
like dogs, cats and even monkeys,
people can sing,
people can laugh,
people can be happy,
people can be sad,
people can draw,
people can write,
people can be beautiful,
people can be ugly,
but it does not matter what they look like outside,
it is what they are like on the inside that counts!

Danielle Fletcher (10)
Ashgrove Primary School

JUST ME

Lurking in the shadows, it's a thing I've never seen,
. . . just me.
Up in the attic, a hole in the ceiling . . . just me.
Howling up and down the stairs . . . just me.
Creeping in the study . . . it's me.
Rattling the toilet chain . . . just me.
I stop and listen, I hear a *hee hee* . . .
Now, that's not me!

Joshua Chisim (9)
Ashgrove Primary School

MY DOG IS SO FAT

My dog is so fat, he can't fit in a school-bag.
My dog is so fat and white, he looks like a plastic bag.
My dog is so fat, when he barks he can't run.
My dog always asks for home-made buns.
My dog is so fat, when we take him for a walk,
he has to sit on a skateboard.
My dog is so fat, that when he barks or talks,
you can't hear him.
My dog is so fat, he can't catch a cat.
My dog is so fat, he can't walk to the bin when his
bed is beside it.
There is only one thing I wish for and that is that
my dog was thin.
My dog is so, so, so fat.

Ashleigh Dornan (10)
Ashgrove Primary School

LIFE

My school is called Ashgrove Primary,
it is the best school.
I have a best friend called Laura,
she has a pet snake called Sliver,
it likes eating crickets and sometimes liver.
My teacher is called Mr Morrow,
he has brown curly hair.
I have got a rabbit called Honey,
who is a funny bunny,
he likes eating chocolate money.
My favourite subject is maths.
When my work is done, I like to watch Taz.

Lynsay Morrison (10)
Ashgrove Primary School

THE ZOO

I love to see the monkeys,
swinging from different trees.
I'm glad they don't keep too many bees.
I once saw an otter,
swimming in the water.
I love to see the elephants,
the gorillas too,
especially baby Naziboo,
but sadly, he's now away
to learn to act the way gorillas play.
The cages are very clean,
when the animals are in them, they can't be seen.
The thing I like most of all
is the gorilla standing so tall.

Stacey Keel (10)
Ashgrove Primary School

MY BIG BAD BRO

My Big Bad Bro is twenty-five,
he has two pairs of glasses and an Indian that's five,
he has a toy dragon called Smokey,
sometimes Andrew calls him Bokey.
Sometimes he dances like Michael Jackson,
he dreams about being a Linfield player, he has no chance.
My brother punches me on the back, I cry in a sack.
Sometimes he spits in my eye, I wish I could make him cry.
He put a spider in my bed, I knew, I felt something crawling
up my leg, then on my knee.
He said 'I didn't know you liked spiders.'
Now that's my Big, Bad, Bro.

Christopher Mehaffey (10)
Ashgrove Primary School

In A Jungle

I come from a jungle
with gorillas and monkeys
that swing about the trees.
I live in a house with parrots
and animals that jump about.

But don't forget, I'm only Neil.
I have a room service.
I swing on some trees
like the monkeys and gorillas do
when they are happy,
but still I don't pat my tummy
when I'm angry.

Neil Whiteside (9)
Ashgrove Primary School

My Rabbit

My rabbit's name is Jessica,
she is grey, white and brown,
and she sometimes acts like a clown.
She has long droopy ears that hang down from her head,
when I take her into my room, she sits on top of my bed.
She runs about in our garage all day long,
when I come home from school I sing her a little song.
When I try to catch her at night to put her in her hutch,
she runs away from me like mad
because she hates going into her hutch.
But I still love her, very, very, much.

Laura Thompson (10)
Ashgrove Primary School

BUT I'M NOT LIKE THAT

People can have blonde hair, short hair,
brown hair or even black hair.
People can have proud, kind mouths.
Some people can have big, sniffy noses,
but I'm not like that!

People can have green beady eyes,
or even helpful caring hands.
Sometimes they can have shaking, knobbly knees,
but I'm not like that!

People can have cold fingers,
or dirty, smelly toes, or even
some have thin bellies,
but I'm not like that!

Abigail Ramsay (9)
Ashgrove Primary School

ON A SNOWY WINTER'S NIGHT

On a snowy, winter's night,
you should wrap yourself up tight,
and hope that the bugs don't bite.
Don't wake up hibernating animals when
they're sleeping until spring.
They are sleeping,
and you should be too.
You should hope the frost won't bite you.
On a winter's night, the dark sky
is like outer space.

Ryan Montgomery (9)
Ashgrove Primary School

FOOTBALL IN THE GARDEN

Football in the garden,
the goal post is our shed.
Father gets really angry
when we tell him the flowers are dead.
'Get that ball, go out of here -
and learn to kick right -
with a bit of skill,
you'll play like Ian Wright.'

Johnathan Chivers (9)
Ashgrove Primary School

WINTER

Winter is cold.
In winter I have to wear gloves
to keep me very warm.
I play snowballs with my sister,
and my sister is very cold,
but I am not - she never gets me.

Charys Anderson (9)
Ashgrove Primary School

SPRING

Singing birds on the treetops,
prancing lambs in the field,
roots are starting to sprout.
I'm out playing in the garden
nearing summer in the sunshine.
Gorgeous flowers are bright.

Holly Cochrane (9)
Ashgrove Primary School

SPRING

It is spring.
The baby birds sing.
The sun is out, it is bright,
the sun is giving us lots of light.
See the rainbow in the sky,
it is red, yellow, blue, green and pink,
the rainbow makes me think
what a lovely day it is!
People playing in fields,
swimming in the ponds,
the flowers growing in the heat,
people going on holiday.
I am going to sleep in my tent tonight.
I can't wait.

Cheryl Keel (10)
Ashgrove Primary School

SUMMER

In summer there's a light blue sky.
In summer little children go and play.
In summer there's a gorgeous bright sun.
In summer there are kind parents looking at the children.
In summer there's a lovely calm sea,
in which grown-ups and children go and swim.
Sailor-men go sailing in a boat.
Eat cool, melty ice-cream, so lovely.
Oh, lovely little birds singing peacefully.
Build sandy sandcastles.
Have fun.

Rayhaanah Ali (9)
Ashgrove Primary School

HOLIDAY

My beautiful young nanny -
I call her granny -
went away to stay
for our holiday.
We went on brilliant, fun, amusements,
we got ice-cream,
it was just like a dream.
We went to see Parent Trap,
and I had a nap,
then at the end I clapped
and so did my nanny.
Then I went up to my bedroom,
I loved Disneyland Paris,
but I really missed my mum's kiss.

Carly Young (9)
Ashgrove Primary School

WINTER

When winter comes it brings snow and rain,
some people say it wrecks their brain.
Children love it, can't you see,
because Santa brings us a pressie.
For my Christmas dinner I had a pie
and looked out at the sky.
I saw white, grey and blue
with some snow coming out too.
When the ground is sparkling white
me and my brother go out and fight,
then we try to make more snowmen.
Later we put our feet on the radiator.

Jonathan Boyd (9)
Ashgrove Primary School

SPRING

Tall, green trees blossom and
happy children play with joy.
Blackbirds sing in the trees as
beautiful coloured flowers grow.
Farm animals have babies.
Tasty chocolate eggs at Easter.

Margaret Watt (9)
Ashgrove Primary School

MY TEACHER

I like my teacher, she is kind,
even when I'm working, she is on my mind.
Her hair is short and thin,
I would never eat out of a tin.
So if you have a teacher and she is kind,
she should always be on your mind.

Natasha Tumilson (8)
Ashgrove Primary School

SCHOOL

Maths and English,
boards and chalk.
People shouting all day long.
Breaktime, lunchtime, all gone now.
Bell is going, mummies all showing,
back tomorrow for another day.

Linzi Ferguson (9)
Ashgrove Primary School

WILDLIFE

The wildlife is large,
the wildlife is beautiful.
When the tiger rushes through the grass
if you stop and think,
you could hear it in your mind.
The elephant, it bangs and bangs
until the grass is nearly broken.

Debra Bell (9)
Ashgrove Primary School

THE SKOOKY NIGHT

One night I was walking down a street,
there was a house that gave me a fright.
I went close to it and something came out.
It was a big, black bat,
it came near me and gave me a fright.
I opened the door and walked in,
there was a man and he was so kind to me.

Joanne Lockhart (9)
Ashgrove Primary School

SPRING

Spring is when the flowers all sprout.
Spring is when the kids come out.
Spring is when everything's new.
Spring is when the cows go *'moo'*.
Spring is when the golden sun
shines down on everyone.

Matthew Boyd (9)
Ashgrove Primary School

CLOUDS

When I look to the sky
the clouds float so high.
Clouds can change size and shape,
the clouds may look like faces
or little men having races.
Sometimes at night I look out
the window, it looks like little men,
dancing and prancing,
but after a while they go away
until the next day.

Rebecca Hamilton (8)
Ashgrove Primary School

CHRISTMASTIME

Christmastime is very good,
it's the season with a lot of food.
Singers coming round the doors,
some of their songs are
shaking the floors.
We are putting up our tree,
my mum, my dad, my sister and me.
I love Christmas, I hope you do,
'cause if you love Jesus,
He'll love you too.

Heather Davidson (8)
Ashgrove Primary School

MY DREAM

I walk upstairs to bed
off to rest my weary head
As I lie down to go to sleep
who should come and have a peep?
Little Willie Winkie and Little Bo Peep,
followed by her flock of sheep.
Who's that knocking on my door?
It's Little Red Riding Hood
with her basket full of goodies galore.
She had missed a turning in the wood
and landed here with her little red hood.
Who's that banging on the stairs?
It's the Grand Old Duke of York and his 10,000 men.
Oh no! Who else?
Ah! It's just my alarm clock on the shelf.
It was a dream, but oh such fun!
Now a new day has begun.

Shauna McCann (11)
Ashgrove Primary School

AUTUMN BREEZE

When the wind blows through your hair
it almost takes you up in the air,
so when the leaves are on the ground
you can go dancing all around.
The autumn breeze
freezes your knees
and makes your little nose sneeze,
so you'll have to stay in your bed
or your nose will turn bright red.

Kirsty McNutt (9)
Ashgrove Primary School

Pancake Tuesday

Pancakes, pancakes everywhere,
even flying through the air.
It's a project for young and old,
it's a legend always told.
Flour, sugar, don't forget milk,
mix it till it's as smooth as silk.
Crack the egg,
on someone's head,
heat up the grill,
they will taste brill.
Get the lemon, start the peeling,
flip it high, but watch the ceiling!
Weigh the sugar on the scales,
the whole taste, it never fails.

Sarah Davidson (11)
Ashgrove Primary School

Alliteration

One orange octopus
Two terrifying tarantulas
Three thrashing thunderbolts
Four ferocious foxes
Five fearless felines
Six slithering snakes
Seven song singing starlings
Eight enormous elephants
Nine not so very attractive newts
Ten tall traffic wardens

Rebecca Ingram (11)
Ashgrove Primary School

SPRING

In spring there's lots of fun,
lots of fun for everyone.
Hello sun, goodbye snow,
sit and watch the daffodils while they glow.
Run away,
go and play
with all your friends.

Lauren Collins (8)
Ashgrove Primary School

MY SCHOOL

My school is so cool,
it has a rule not to act so cool.
My mum says it's not cool
to break the rule in school,
but at the end of the day,
my school is okay.

Hannah Carmichael (9)
Ashgrove Primary School

LONELINESS

Loneliness is blue,
it tastes like soggy chips
and sounds like rain falling
and vibrating in puddles.
It's like you're trapped somewhere
without any friends.

Suzi Bradley (10)
Ballymacash Primary School

OUTSIDE

Outside is full of owls and shadows,
people talking and shouting,
figures creeping silently,
shapes standing in stillness,
shadows like bears,
bats flapping.

Outside is full of creepy shadows,
owls flying restlessly,
moles moving quickly,
eyes looking creepily for work,
cats miaowing,
owls hooting.

Outside is full of frightening movement,
howling from all the bats,
weird movements running up and down,
moles creeping around silently,
figures moving,
bats screeching.

Julie Stewart (11)
Ballymacash Primary School

FEAR

Fear is white.
It tastes like freezing cold water,
it smells like a million blocks of ice,
it looks like ten large lions in jail with you,
it sounds live wolves howling,
it feels like a robber in your house with a gun.

Christopher Richmond (10)
Ballymacash Primary School

HAMSTER

A hamster is fat
and a small animal,
a soft, wee thing.
he lives in a cage
and he nibbles at nuts.
But in his cage he has a wheel.
He sleeps in a furry bed
and he is so cute and round.

I wish I had one in my house,
to play with me,
but my mum would not let me get one.

Richard Hanna (8)
Ballymacash Primary School

HAPPINESS

Happiness is yellow,
it tastes like fresh strawberries,
it smells like lovely red roses,
out in a summer field.
Happiness looks like the sun which
rises in the east,
sounds like the little birds
singing in the trees we see.
Happiness feels like I'm flying
and watching the birds pass me.

Christopher Morrow (10)
Ballymacash Primary School

ROGER THE HORSE

Roger is black,
but very greedy and never stops eating.
he is wild and if you don't take
control, he'll surely run away.

Playful but naughty,
fast and jumps high,
he will play all day
if you dare let him try.

His stable is number four
and he shares with Star.
You can spot him from afar,
the hungry champion.

Roger the Wonder Horse,
instead of Champion the Wonder Horse,
trots away that very day.
The best little horse that was ever born.

Angela Champion (8)
Ballymacash Primary School

ANGER

Anger is black,
it tastes like smoke from a bonfire,
and it smells like burning wood.
Anger looks like an explosion
and sounds like a big bomb.
Anger is a hot fire and if you touch it,
you will get burnt.

Deborah McCarthy (11)
Ballymacash Primary School

CAT

When I got my cat it ran about the house,
it purred and purred and purred.
It ran across the room.
She drank all her milk,
she ate all her food,
she jumped on my knee.
I thought I'd make her happy
by buying her a mouse,
she ate him and she was so happy,
I called her Prance.

Hannah Kelly (8)
Ballymacash Primary School

MY FRIEND MILLY THE HORSE

Have you met my friend Milly?
She is a horse.
She has a whit coat.
She is a beautiful horse.
I ride her every Saturday.

Gary Keep (8)
Ballymacash Primary School

MY BUZZY BUMBLEBEE

My little bumblebee plays all the time.
It eats honey once a day.
It likes the sun, but not the rain.
When it comes out to play, we all run away.

Arlene Robinson (10)
Ballymacash Primary School

MONKEY

A monkey swings on branches to get bananas.
It climbs up trees.
A monkey is a naughty animal.
A long tail is for hanging upside down
on the trees.
Baby monkeys are funny to play with.
The skin is hairy on a monkey.
I would name my monkey after my teacher.

Sharon Magee (8)
Ballymacash Primary School

SNAKE

A snake is slimy and wriggly.
It can bite and hiss and stretch out long.
Snakes wrap around you
and squeeze you tight.
Snakes are frightening,
they scare you when they move so fast.

Matthew McCarthy (9)
Ballymacash Primary School

HAMSTERS

Hamsters are playful,
they play on the wheel.
They're cute and soft,
they play in their cages all day.
They are clever and noisy,
they nibble their food all the time.

They are very fluffy,
they are cute and warm.
They watch TV in the living room.
They sleep all day and wake all night.
Some hamsters are thin and some are fat.

Cheryl McClean (9)
Ballymacash Primary School

Rabbit

I have a rabbit
who has a bushy tail.
He is called Snowy.
He eats carrots and cabbage all day long.
He has big, floppy ears.
Snowy drinks water.
Snowy is playful.
He lets you stroke his head.
He is my pet.

Ashlene Dalzell (8)
Ballymacash Primary School

Dogs

At night, my dog scrapes the window for some food.
He always dirties the window when he scrapes it.
Dogs bark at strangers,
all night long.
We can't get to sleep, sleep, sleep.
The dogs chase the cats.
My dog even chases the birds in the sky.

Kassandera Patton (8)
Ballymacash Primary School

MY DOG

My dog is cute.
Sometimes she is annoying
because she always cuts holes in bags
so she can get at the food.
My dog had puppies,
she always keeps an eye on them.
My dog can run faster than Linford Christie.

Jason Haydon (8)
Ballymacash Primary School

WHALES

Whales are big.
Whales are small.
Whales are always growing.
Whales are grey.
Whales are black and white too.
Whales are always playful,
and friendly too.

Ryan Lynn (9)
Ballymacash Primary School

DOLPHINS

Dolphins are very intelligent like you and me.
They are very cute.
They jump out of the water and dive back in again.
They are graceful when they swim about.
They make funny noises like *eeeeee, aaaaaaaa*.
I think they sing and chat, just like us.

Lisa McLaren (9)
Ballymacash Primary School

My Little Turtle

My little turtle is slow on his feet.
He's tiny and sweet and green.
My little turtle is faster than a snail.
He has got little teeth.
He's the quietest turtle of them all,
but he's not quiet when he's eating.

Hayley Topping (10)
Ballymacash Primary School

What Are Animals?

Animals come in all different sizes.
Some are *huge*,
some are small,
like a mouse and an elephant.
Loads are really cute
and loads are very scary too.

Rachael McCord (9)
Ballymacash Primary School

The Tiger

I am the tiger.
I can get my prey.
I can fetch a piece of meat.
I am fierce,
I can attack a human.

Michaela Robinson (9)
Ballymacash Primary School

THE TIGER

The tiger has very sharp teeth
and a very long, stripy tail.
He roars at you
if you are bad,
and he eats you up.

Arran Crossey (9)
Ballymacash Primary School

WINTER

Winter, winter, there you are,
your time has come at last.
Don't hide, don't cry, you are my hero,
so spread that snow and do your stuff.
Don't let time waste away,
you have to save the day!

See the little children play and play,
all day. Then it's teatime, the
children are called to fill their
tummies full. So spread your snow
now to make more snow to play,
play, play all day.

So now it's time to say farewell,
why, why, oh why do we have
to say goodbye, so now you have
to go away. I hope spring will
come and save the day!

Joanna Cushnahan (8)
Ballymacward Primary School

Autumn Colours

In the autumn there I play.
In the garden, that's where I'll stay.
All the colours of a rainbow,
green, red, brown and yellow.

After a hard day's work
my daddy sits down and starts to ponder.
Should he go and start again.
To rake the leaves all over.

I go out to throw these colours all about.
In a big pond of colours I jump and play.
I hope it will stay
in my back garden for another day!

Orla Hagan (9)
Ballymacward Primary School

Winter

I like winter
because you can
splash and jump,
skip and play.
Winter is cold,
winter is white,
the trees are bare.
When the flakes come down,
it's time to play.
I get on my sleigh.

Martin McGarry (7)
Ballymacward Primary School

One Misty Day

I see the children
play in the cold and
misty weather. They
jump and jump till their
cold has gone.

The weather is very
cold and misty
but the children still
do not care.

Now the mist has
gone and the little
children sing loudly and
people come round.

The children breathe
out cold, misty breath
and grow colder and
colder.

Carla Mulholland (8)
Ballymacward Primary School

Winter

In winter the snow comes,
Jack Frost comes too.
I say Mummy, Mummy
the snow has come. And I throw
snow at my sister and she
throws snow at me too.

Ashleen Mulholland (8)
Ballymacward Primary School

THE SNOWY DAY

One wild day
drizzling with snow
how fun it was
watching it fall down slowly.

How the wind blew,
tapping roughly
down my back, wildly
as it hit my feet and tickled.

It became night and I
had to go home freezing
with the bitter ice
so slowly and gently frosting over.

I got into my nice warm bed
and fell asleep quietly
dreaming of another
wild and snowy day.

Clara McStravick (9)
Ballymacward Primary School

SUMMER BLUE DAY

One summer blue day
the heat is like gold.
The trees are green as can be,
the grass is like a green, green frog.
The sun is like a fire.
I see the trees sway from side to side.
The lake is like a prickly star . . .
I love summer blue days.

Kevin Higgins (8)
Ballymacward Primary School

A Windy Day

On a windy day
I looked out my window.
Then I had to say
come out to play.
I go out to play
seeing the leaves falling.
When I come into
the house I see
the wind blowing.
I see the grass turning
lighter green.
I see the trees
bare and freezing cold.

Mark Lynch (8)
Ballymacward Primary School

One Warm Day

The golden sun
pours down on me
like raindrops.
The golden sun stings
my face like boiling hot water.
The sun shines brightly
down on me
and makes a golden band.
I lift a leaf, it sizzles
as I squeeze it in my hand.

Fiona Hagan (8)
Ballymacward Primary School

MY WARM DAY

My warm day was when . . .
the sun blasted my body.
I went to lie on the grass.

I went to sleep and the heat
was like a hot water bottle
peeling at my skin.
I played in the garden
I tumbled and jumped
and wished I was freezing
but I'm still hot.

When the sun went down
I was too cold.
I wished for more.
The sun went down
like a ship sinking under the sea.

Jonathan Jones (8)
Ballymacward Primary School

THE DRIPPING DAY

One day I looked,
out of my window I
saw the dripping rain.
It fell from the sky
like a pot of magic gold.

I have a dream that
it floats but when I
wake up there are
only puddles.

Bernadette Goan (9)
Ballymacward Primary School

WORMS!

Sticky short fuzzy worms,
Long gooey slimy worms,
5cm plump pink worms,
There's lots of worms in the world!

Sticky short wriggly worms,
Long straight slimy worms,
5cm curly pink worms,
There's lots of worms in the world!

Sticky short worms pushing up the soil,
Long slimy worms dragging it all around,
5cm pink worms breaking it all up,
There's lots of worms in the world!

Worms in the ground,
Worms in the soil,
Worms crawling everywhere,
There's lots of worms in the world!

Lynne McCosh (10)
Broughshane Primary School

THE SEA

The sea is rough
The sea goes *ssshhh*
The sea crashes
The sea bangs.

The sea is wavy
The waves go *slosh, slosh*
The sea rolls
The sea is full of fish.

The sea is big
The sea jumps
The waves sway
The sea is great fun.

The sea is deep
The sea is dangerous
The sea moves
The sea can harm people.

Lee Murphy (9)
Broughshane Primary School

HOW I LEARNED TO FLY

One day I was walking down a little path
I heard some birds singing up above my head
I thought I heard one talk to me
I wasn't really sure so I shouted out
'Hey! Were you talking to me?'
The bird said 'Yes'
I said 'I must be dreaming'
I shouted 'What do you want from me?'
The bird said 'Do you want to learn to fly?'
'Sure I do, when can we start?'
'Why not now?'
'Ok' I said.
And they all came down beside me
One of the birds touched me with its wings
And said 'You've got a magical power to fly'
And they all said 'You have to say fly away'
So I did and there I was flying with the birds
And that is how I learned to fly.

Kristi Robinson (9)
Broughshane Primary School

Egyptian Homes

Once I went to Egypt,
To stay with family and friends,
They lived in a small house,
Made from mud and stone.

I stayed with them for quite a bit,
But then I went and split,
I went to stay with friends,
They were very rich,
Their pig lived in a ditch.

They had a servants' block,
Their rooms were bright and airy,
Once I lost my way,
On a very hot day.

I made a hut out of sand and stone,
I spent the night there,
I nearly died without air,
I slept there through the night,
And that was my night-time fright.

Mark Foster (9)
Broughshane Primary School

Mr Oh Mo

Mr Oh Mo got lost in the snow
He looked to the left and the right
What did he see down past his knee
But the long-lost garden hoe.

Mr Oh Mo got lost in the wood
He looked everywhere, up and down
What did he see down past his knee
But the ground on which he stood.

Mr Oh Mo got lost in the pond
He looked to the back and the front
What did he see down past his knee
But the ducks of which he was fond.

Joe Adams (9)
Broughshane Primary School

HORSES

Horseshoes are lucky
And so are horses
That's what I think
And I hope so do you.

Horses in the fields
Horses at the fair
Horses at the merry-go-round
Horses everywhere.

Horses are cute, cuddly and furry
They come in various colours and sizes
But my mum and dad won't let me have one
Although I really wish I did.

I like to ride horses
But I'm sometimes scared
Because I think I'm going to fall off
It usually doesn't turn out that way.

They run races
But I hardly ever watch them
I would race, race, race, and race
If I ever had one.

Megan Lennox (9)
Broughshane Primary School

EGYPTIAN WAYS

The Nile is their water source
It is their farming ground
Their pyramids point up to the sky
And their jewels are made of gold
In the summer they shave their heads.

April is their harvesting season
When doing hot, dirty jobs
Men wear a kilt
And women wear a short skirt
Noblemen wear pleated kilts.

And noblewomen wear flowing, pleated dresses.
Wraps and cloaks are worn in winter.
Some nobles wear beaded dresses
People often go barefoot
Their shoes are made of reeds.

If I were there
I'd search for tombs
And examine the Pyramids.

Gordon Davidson (9)
Broughshane Primary School

COLOURS

Red is the colour of blood
and the lovely race.

Blue is the water sparkling
in the sun,
and my school jumper.

Green is the alligator
and the leaves on the tree.

Black is the coal mined from the ground
and the starless night.

Yellow is the summer sun
and my cousin's hair.

Ian Mark (9)
Broughshane Primary School

OWLS

Owls, owls, owls
They sleep all day
They come out at night
Owls . . . owls . . . owls

Owls, owls, owls
They hoot all night
They have lots of fun at night
Owls, owls, owls

Owls, owls, owls
They have parties in the air
But at the break of dawn they stop
Owls . . . owls . . . owls

Owls, owls, owls
At the break of dawn they go back into their trees
And sleep all day
Owls, owls, owls

Owls, owls, owls
While they're sleeping we are eating
But while we are sleeping they are eating
Owls, owls, owls.

Joanne Currie (10)
Broughshane Primary School

Dogs

I like dogs,
They have nice fur,
And they also like to chase cats,
But the worst thing about them is,
They bark,
I like dogs,
They can stick the cold,
But I can
I also wonder how they sniff things out,
I like dogs,
I like to take dogs for walks,
But do they?
I wonder how they eat so quick,
I can't,
I like dogs!

Dean Campbell (9)
Broughshane Primary School

Football

F is for football, the game I like to play
O is for offside
O is for out when the ball is past the line
T is for throw-in when the ball goes out
B is for ball that we play with
A is for acrobatic overhead kick
L is for long range when I shoot from afar
L is for Liverpool my favourite team.

Jason Clyde (9)
Broughshane Primary School

THE SKY AND SPACE

The sun is rising from his bed
High in the sky he climbs higher and higher
Until the night comes swooping by
The stars come out and play about in the night sky.

Mars and Pluto, Mercury and Earth are some of
The planets in our universe
There are hundreds of galaxies
Millions of millions of stars all up in space.

Rockets being launched
Comets flying through space
At over 1000 miles an hour
The sky is full of things
That we've never, ever seen.

Ruarcc McAloon (9)
Broughshane Primary School

ICE HOCKEY

I is for ice rink that the players skate on
C is for checking someone onto the boards
E is for enormous body-check through the glass.

H is for hockey stick for passing the puck
O is for Ottawa Arena in Canada
C is for the crowd cheering
K is for the keeper, minding his net
E is for Ed Belfore, an ice hockey keeper
Y is for the yawning open net.

Aaron Bailie (9)
Broughshane Primary School

COOKIE

Cookie is my guinea-pig
He's like a big ball of fluff
But when I give him a carrot to eat,
He just can't have enough.

He wanders round the cage,
With his friend Honey
And now he's come to old age,
He looks so cute and fluffy.

I like him when he's lively
And I like him when he's calm
It doesn't seem that long ago,
Since he was the size of my palm.

I've had good fun with Cookie,
Though I knew this day would come,
When Cookie simply slips away,
And now there's no more fun.

Andrea McNeill (9)
Broughshane Primary School

WINTER

Winter, my favourite time of all,
Coming out of autumn,
Coming through to winter,
Soon the snow will fall.

Making snowmen with the snow,
Having snowball fights,
Skating on the ice,
The really cold air that floats by,
Me again and again.

Now we're coming into spring,
The sun is coming out,
The snowman has disappeared,
The flowers are coming,
The colours have come again.

Richard Allen (9)
Broughshane Primary School

EGYPT

Pyramids, palm trees,
Deserts, so very hot,
Take a trip to Egypt
And I'm sure you'll see a lot!

The land around the River Nile
Is their only ground for crops,
Working and digging every day,
Although there were no shops.

Jewellery was always used
By both rich and poor,
I don't know how the poor got theirs
That, I'm not sure.

There are many places to go and see
Wherever you step it's history,
Five thousand year old pyramids
It seems all like a mystery.

Egypt is a beautiful country,
With many things to see.

Howard Jamieson (9)
Broughshane Primary School

EGYPTIANS

Kings when they died had tombs built
There came in hand a new style of
Pyramids the step pyramids.
They could reach the stars at night.
People were stealing stuff from the Pyramids.

The houses were built in towns or villages
The bricks were made from dried mud
They kept houses cool because the windows were big
Rich people would have a pool
Poor people did not have a pool.

Some people wore wigs to parties
In Egypt there is the River Nile
It floods every year
After the flood every year there is new mud.

Jennifer Millar (9)
Broughshane Primary School

EGYPTIANS

I saw the River Nile
And I saw the people's style
The Pyramids were huge
The mummies were so scary
The River Nile is the biggest river.

We had to walk a mile
To get to the Nile
We saw a lot of palm trees
We got honey from the bees.

I saw a Pharaoh
And a farm
It was really warm.

Richard Montford (9)
Broughshane Primary School

TO THE FUTURE

As I gaze out my window,
Into the starry sky,
I can see into the future.

There in space,
There are people travelling,
On jet scooters to the moon.

I also see monsters from Mars,
Hopping into space cars,
To come to the Earth.

Back on Earth,
The kids all have robots,
To do their schoolwork for them.

Some scientists
Have lifted the Titanic's hull
From its watery grave.

The people on Earth,
Are paid for . . . well,
Absolutely nothing.

Was this a dream?
Or maybe
It really is the future.

Lisa Douglas (10)
Broughshane Primary School

THE EGYPTIANS

The Egyptian kings had tombs,
And their palaces had many rooms.
They built pyramids and they were grand,
While their children played in the sand.

There is a river called The Nile,
And it floods for half a mile.
The Egyptian people are unkind,
But very wise in the mind.

Some people were wealthy,
And very healthy.
The Egyptians have gold,
And some are very bold.

The farmers are working in their fields,
While the army used their shields.
The Egyptian people have slaves,
But never keep them in caves.

Whenever a Pharaoh died,
All of the people cried.
But that's not all,
Some people sighed.

Peter Kennedy (9)
Broughshane Primary School

AN EGYPTIAN POEM

When it was sunny
Egyptians brought round their friends
And paddled in the pool
Or sunbathed in the gardens.

The Egyptians' windows were small and tight
But they also let in air and light.
Thick walls helped to keep houses cool,
A rich man would have used his pool (to keep cool).

Lisa-Jane Millar (9)
Broughshane Primary School

BUGS!

Bugs are sometimes funny looking
Sometimes they get in your way
Sometimes they give you a big, hairy, scary look
But some bugs just slither away.

Some bugs are busy, like ants
Ladybirds are spotty and they fly
Worms help gardeners by slithering through the soil
Butterflies, beautifully coloured, fly high.

Caterpillars are hairy but cute
Slugs are slimy and fat
Bookworms are full of all kinds of information
Including every little detail about cats.

Frogs eat flies, flies are very, very small
Bees buzz about and sting
Spiders are scary, with eight long legs
Grasshoppers hop and rub their wings to sing.

Bugs are sometimes funny looking
Sometimes they get in your way
Sometimes they give you a big, hairy scary look
But some bugs just slither away

Sarah Kernohan (10)
Broughshane Primary School

A Life In Egypt

Once a year,
River Nile,
Had heavy rains and melting snow,
Which made the river overflow.

Farmers ploughed and sowed their fields,
While the armies used their shields,
The main crops were wheat and barley
Barley was also made into beer.

The Egyptians wrote on paper called papyrus,
Which was made from river reeds,
Boys went to school,
If they were lazy, they were punished
With a beating.

Girls stayed home in Egypt,
And were taught by their mothers.

Schools were for boys
Who came from wealthy homes.
Schools were next to temples.
Teachers were priests.

Dar Óma McAloon (8)
Broughshane Primary School

My Feline Friend

My feline friend is ginger and white,
And his name is Billy.
He's always there to meet me,
As faithful as a human friend.
He's always in the middle of everything I do,
Always wanting to know what's going on.

Though he's getting old,
He's as curious as a kitten,
He isn't as energetic as he used to be,
But still he's full of fun,
I love my feline friend,
He's just the perfect pet!

Suzanne Smyth (10)
Broughshane Primary School

THE MILLENNIUM BUG!

I imagine
the Millennium Bug,
as a grey or silver machine
with long claws and big, sharp teeth
my Millennium Bug.

I imagine,
the Millennium Bug,
as a machine that will shut down computers
or maybe cut off the power
my Millennium Bug.

I imagine
the Millennium Bug,
as a machine which will demolish everything
I'll make sure he doesn't destroy my computer
I hope he'll just stay my Millennium Bug.,

I imagine
the Millennium Bug . . .

Loise Boyd (10)
Broughshane Primary School

A Chinese Kangaroo

I've had cats and dogs
and miniature frogs
And I've kept the odd snail too.
But never, ever have I ever had a Chinese kangaroo.

I've had a loving dove
that went into a glove
and found a friend called Flee.
But never, ever have I ever had a Chinese kangaroo.

I've had rats and mice
and they've gobbled up rice
they've had the odd pizza as well.
But never, ever have I ever had a Chinese kangaroo.

Gemma McClenaghan (10)
Broughshane Primary School

There's A Monster Under My Bed

There's a monster under my bed, my bed
It bumps and romps
I tried to shoot it dead
But he ate all the Flumps.

There's a monster under my bed, my bed
It scares me when I am sleeping
He wakes me up in the middle of the night
With all his yelling and thumping.

There's a monster under my bed, my bed
But when the morning light shines so bright
He's not too keen on my mum.
So he keeps out of sight until night.

Philip McBurney (9)
Broughshane Primary School

EGYPT

Egypt is a hot, dry place
In summer Egyptians shaved their hair
Long cloaks and kilts that's what Egyptians wear.

Farming does not seem fun
They plough and sow their fields
Fields were small
When the summer comes it floods them all.

The River Nile was their water source
When the flood came
It washed up soil and grain
While that happened they made and fixed sculptures.

They wore anklets, earrings and girdles
The anklets were made out of gold
The earrings were introduced in the New Kingdom.

Stuart Kennedy (9)
Broughshane Primary School

WINTER

Hard white snow
Crunch, snow, crunch
Covers things
Smothers things
Makes things
White.

Tanya Wilson (8)
Broughshane Primary School

Food

Food is commendable for you,
It's healthy, nutritious and tasty,
It makes you fit and ready for anything,
Food is for you!

There are three meals for you,
Breakfast, lunch and dinner,
Tasty meals they all are,
But if you eat them all at once, you will get a vexed tummy.

Some types of foods are vegetables and fruit,
Fruits are apples, bananas, pears and oranges,
Vegetables are carrots, onions, sprouts and cabbage,
Fruits are a nice snack.

The question is what foods do you like?

Mark Loughridge (9)
Broughshane Primary School

Bear Hunt Race

We are going on a bear hunt,
Oh! How exciting it will be,
We're going to catch a big one,
It will be fluffy and lovely to see.

Look I've found some footprints,
Big, big ones, come look and see.
I think I hear something.
Ah! It's a bear running after me.
Ah! Ah! Ah! Please don't let it eat me.
    It did.

Jane Burgess (8)
Broughshane Primary School

CRAZY MRS BROWN

Crazy Mrs Brown, in her dressing gown
Hanging from the window sill
Dusting away
While she sang a merry old tune.

The very next day she flew to the moon
On her broom
On the way down she went into a bush
Eating a bag of Flumps.

Crazy Mrs Brown, she hid in a cupboard
With the key closed in
She sat in the corner and stayed right there
Never to be seen
                Again!

Patricia Boyd (9)
Broughshane Primary School

THE SEA

The sea is big
The sea is great
The sea is full of fish.

The sea is rough
The sea is dangerous
The sea can harm people.

The sea is a perfect world
The sea is very deep
The sea is great fun.

Aaron Doyle (8)
Broughshane Primary School

GROW UP

Grow up, grow up, you're being silly.
Go and play with your friend Billy.
Grow up, grow up, stop being lazy
Go and play, stop being crazy.
Grow up, grow up, I don't know why
Being young is such a tie.

Slow down, slow down, you're getting too tall
Your clothes soon won't fit you at all.
Slow down, slow down, you're eating too much
You can't keep on eating Monster Munch.
Slow down, slow down, it's always called back
It's too much for a young girl to take.

Stop it, stop it, you're growing too old,
No longer will you do as you're told.
Stop it, stop it, life soon passes by
Now it's time to remember and cry.
Stop it, stop it, time passes on,
Life will soon be over and done.
Stop it, stop it, I look at the sun,
Being old is not much fun.

Keri Smyth (9)
Broughshane Primary School

MY DOG

My dog is called Mike
and he likes to play on his bike.
But sometimes he can be
a little bit noisy.

I always tell him 'Don't sit by that fire,
you'll get a bit of sizzle.
Go out to the rain and
get a bit of drizzle.'

Christina Fleck (9)
Broughshane Primary School

SPONGE AND SPIKER

Sponge and Spiker grew a peach,
And divided up some pennies each.
It came from a tree,
That no one could see,
Because the peach was so big.

James, the nephew,
Hated them so.
Everyone else did too,
Except Tubby Po.

Sponge said Spiker was such a pain,
James just felt like going insane.
They pushed and shoved him,
And treated him like dust,
I'll tell you what I'd do,
I'd jump on a bus.

Sponge and Spiker seem so bad,
When they get killed,
We'll all be glad.
Soon they'll be dead,
Just wait and see,
If they die tomorrow
We'll be jumping with glee.

Nigel Elliott (8)
Broughshane Primary School

EGYPT

The country of Egypt is very dirty
And you go on bare feet or sandals
You should keep your feet clean
The mud is the worst I've ever seen.

There are two types of pyramids
The step and the straight
So inside the tomb the people lay
The step pyramid was built to
Help the spirits on their way.

The god Osiris, is the god of dead
Re, the sun god, has an eagle head
Amun is the god of all
Bes, the child god, is very small.

Mark McNeill (8)
Broughshane Primary School

MY MUM AND DAD

I love my mum and dad,
Sometimes they get really mad.
My dad is a lad,
My mum is very glad.

Sometimes they get very sad,
They get mad if we are bad.
My dad has no money
But he loves bread and honey.

My mum had a bun,
And she ate it in the sun.
My mum is very lucky,
My dad is always plucky.

My dad loves his coffee,
My mum has some toffee.
My dad has some hens,
He keeps them in little pens.

Gemma Eaton (8)
Buick Memorial Primary School

My Dog

My dog is crazy,
And is as fresh as a daisy.
It plays with me,
It loves the sea.

It is bad sometimes,
It loves to climb.
It is brown,
It loves to climb down.
It is nine,
And it is mine!

It loves its food,
It is good.
It loves bones,
The same as I like ice-cream cones.
It is sad,
But it is not bad.

It is my friend,
It does not like to go round a bend,
It is my dog,
It had a pup called Nog.

James Matthew Fenton (7)
Buick Memorial Primary School

MY DOG

My little dog is called Ben,
He loves my little hen.
Very loudly he howls,
At the little brown owls.

He loves his food,
His kennel is made of wood.
He loves to run,
And likes to eat a bun.

Ben and I go for a walk,
We can hear the people talk.
Ben and I have such fun,
Out in the bright midday sun!

One day I was outside,
Ben and I were playing on the slide.
I sat on my swing,
And heard all the birds sing.

Ben was covered in mud,
There was a little flower with a bud.
I gave Ben a treat,
He loves a juicy bone to eat.

We found a little fox,
In a small, tiny box.
It was brown,
Ben had a frown.

I took it to the house,
Where there was a little grey mouse.
We let the fox go,
Then it started to snow.

Elaine Campbell (8)
Buick Memorial Primary School

My Mum

My mum is nice,
And she is afraid of mice.
She saw a mouse,
And ran out of the house.

She has brown hair,
When she shouts, she gives me a scare!
When I am bad,
My mum goes mad!

I love my mum,
And she likes to hum.
My mum loves to watch Coronation Street,
But she does not like to eat Shredded Wheat.

My mum and I are good friends,
That fun we have will never end.
My mum cooks my dinner,
And if I do not eat it, I will get thinner!

I like to eat my food,
I think my mum is very good.
I do not like it when my mum gets mad,
It makes me feel very sad.

Ashley McIlroy (8)
Buick Memorial Primary School

MY BEST FRIENDS

One of my friends is Johnny,
even though he's grumpy, he's still my friend.
Lee is my friend too,
even though he's dopey, I hope he doesn't see this!
My other friend is another Lee,
but he's the smartest one.
Adrian is a good friend too,
he is a footballer as well
And we're all jealous of him.
I've got other friends too,
but these friends are the best.
Sometimes we fall out,
but we get back together quite soon.
I don't know where I would be
without my best friends.

Andrew Linton (11)
Cloughmills Primary School

MY DOG HARVEY

I get up early to feed my dog
Then out on the chain he goes.
Running around and around the drain
He barks to call his friend
Over to play with him.
Then scratches at the door to come in out of the cold.
When he comes in he goes to sleep.
He is a Jack Russell terrier
He has a funny face and a nice cuddly coat.
He's playful and my friend.
I love him just as much as I love my sister.

Alex Hunter (9)
Cloughmills Primary School

THE UNINVITED GUEST

This hairy rat came into the kitchen.
It was in the vegetable rack.
The carrots he came out of
And he was that fat he could hardly get through the door.
He was that fat that when my sister came into the kitchen
The rat sat so still she thought it was a teddy bear
And went over and hugged it.
Then he was ticklish in the neck.
Then my mum came over too
And she knew it was a real rat.
So she shouted at Suzanne to get away
Then she got a brush and hurt it
And that was all.

Adrian Boyd (8)
Cloughmills Primary School

MY DAD

My dad is a bossy boots
He bosses me around
He says 'Switch on the television
And get me the salt.'
He makes me work too hard.
He gives me a hard time all day long.
He never gives me a break.
Although he lets me watch television
He always makes me work
I never get to play
Poor old me.
What a life!

David Adams (8)
Cloughmills Primary School

The Foal

Tender-eyed, young and sweet,
Just a foal on unsure feet.
Nestling close to his wise mother,
To this one horse,
He knows no other.
Running free and having fun,
No cares yet, for this little one.

Holly Matthews (11)
Cloughmills Primary School

My Big Sister

My sister is nice to me,
but other times she just bullies me.
Takes me into town,
and pretends she is a queen with a crown.
Shouts at me and sits on me
and always makes me weak at the knee.

Ashley Kirker (11)
Cloughmills Primary School

My Granny

My gran is big, my gran is fat
I made my gran a lovely hat.
My gran has a dog and some cats
And they sleep on her good mat.
I love my granny, I do, I do
And she loves me more than you.

Naomie Campbell (10)
Cloughmills Primary School

My Dad

My dad is a bossy boots.
He tells me to 'Put on the TV,
get the beer from the fridge,
put the salt in the cupboard.'
Sometimes I like my dad.
He can be nice sometimes.
I like it when we have a bit of fun.
I would like it if he was nicer.
My dad can be a bit angry.

Natasha Linton (8)
Cloughmills Primary School

My Teachers

I like my teachers.
My teachers are very nice to us.
They do lots of nice things with us.
We get to play games.
They let us sit beside our friends
They have got lots of good ideas.
My teacher lets us make a story book.
Sometimes she says 'Get on with your work,
Don't talk to the person beside you.'

Stacey McFetridge (10)
Cloughmills Primary School

MY DOG

My dog is a bearded collie.
She is called Shep.
My dog has a scruffy old beard.
She looks a bit like my grandad.
She sometimes gets excited and bites me.
My dog is nearly as big as me.
Sometimes she jumps on me and makes me fall over.
My dog, what a pet! She never gets upset.
That dog of mine, it never gets tired.
If she gets a hold of my sister's teddies
She rips them to bits.
And my old dog just will not sit.
That old dog of mine, what a pet!

Lee Shannon (10)
Cloughmills Primary School

SPRING

Spring is the beginning of a new year,
Winter's over so there's no need to fear.
Crocuses, daffodils and snowdrops all growing,
Even though all around it is snowing.
All the bells are ringing,
And lots of birds are singing.
They're building their nests,
Far out in the west,
And that's why I think spring is the best.

Susie Houston (11)
Cloughmills Primary School

MY TEACHER

My teacher is very sweet to me.
She never is really grumpy.
When you say 'Oh I forgot to do my homework.'
She always says 'You can do it tomorrow night.'
I feel like saying to her 'Oh you are a hero.'
The boys are very bad.
Mrs Boyd has to scold the boys all the time.
The girls are really good.
Mrs Boyd says always that the girls are very good.
Mrs Boyd and our school have even decided to let us do up the library.
We might even be on School Around The Corner.

Lyndsey Rock (10)
Cloughmills Primary School

A LITTLE BLUE CORSA

A little blue Corsa with alloy wheels.
A sporty car it is indeed.
It has three doors, it's a sporty car.
It's baby blue, it's my favourite colour.
It is for me but not my mother.
She likes the car with five doors.
But doesn't like the colour.
My sister thinks it's cool and so do I.
When I grow up and learn to drive,
I want a baby blue Corsa.

Leanne Strange (11)
Cloughmills Primary School

SHOPPING

In my shopping trolley I put;
One strawberry yoghurt, I don't like peach ones.
Two bags of potatoes, not cold chips.
Three loaves of bread because I want some toast.
Four cartons of milk, not sour milk.
Five tins of peas, garden peas for me please.
Six smelly fish, from the sea.
Seven brown pancakes, very well cooked.
Eight bottles of Coke that are full.
Nine fat turkeys for my Christmas dinner.
Ten rolls of bacon for my dad.
        That will do for today.

Laura Millar (10)
Cloughmills Primary School

IN MY TROLLEY

In my trolley I put;
One big and slimy, electric eel,
Two giant, fire-breathing dragons,
Three small and hairy tarantulas,
Four massive great white sharks,
Five martial arts donkeys,
Six advanced blue whales,
Seven expensive cobras,
Eight very, very, clever iguanas,
Nine little, creepy crawlies,
Ten shy but playful monkeys.

Colin Givens (10)
Cloughmills Primary School

MY DOG

My dog is called Sparky.
He is a Jack Russell terrier.
He is as quick as a spark.
You can see his little white chin in the dark.
He loves playing with my ball.
When I try to catch him he makes me fall.
I love Sparky when he sits on my knee.
Everyone can see that Sparky's the dog for me.

Michaela McKnight (11)
Cloughmills Primary School

MY TWO BROTHERS

My two brothers can be really annoying. They wreck my room.
My baby brother is very funny, he's cute and nice, he's fun too.
My other brother is funny, cute, nice and fun too.
My brother has a PlayStation,
What I hate most is when he takes the controllers off me.
My baby brother comes and bounces on me in the mornings.
But I really love my two brothers.

Rebecca Sweetlove (9)
Cloughmills Primary School

SUMMER

Summer is my favourite time of year
it's nice and hot, relaxing in the sun,
eating an ice-cream. It's just fun.
Eating a nutritious and delicious apple,
Yum, yum, yum!

Pauline McDonald (10)
Cloughmills Primary School

SPRING

Frogspawn in ponds
Lambs in fields
Me in the garden
Daffodils on lawns
Everyone's out and about, and why?
Of course, spring's here!

The sun's in the sky,
Dad's cutting the grass.
Back and forth I swing.
Cute little chicks are hatching out.
Everyone's out and about, and why?
Of course, spring's here again!

Rachel Hanna (8)
Harmony Hill Primary School

DOGS

Dogs are cuddly,
Dogs are cute,
Dogs are fluffy,
And they go 'Woof, woof, woof.'

Some dogs bark,
Some not at all,
Some are very big,
Some, really small.

Some dogs are white,
Some dogs are black,
Do you know what some dogs like to do?
They like to chase the cats!

Alice Moffitt (11)
Harmony Hill Primary School

JUNGLE ANIMALS

Tigers, big and strong, he hunts by day and night.
Has lots of strips that shine at night
And eyes that glow in the dark.

Lions, kings of the jungle, big and bold
He is the boss in his household.
He watches his prey all day long, ready to pounce.
His cubs are waiting for their father to come home.

Elephants, big and strong, big, long trunks with great big ears,
Huge big feet to glide along
Be careful you don't get stood upon.

Monkeys, swing through the jungle from tree to tree.
Bananas on every tree
Very tempting for those monkeys you see.

Victoria Irving (9)
Harmony Hill Primary School

THE FOUR SEASONS

In winter it is cold,
Many Christmas trees are sold.
In spring the plants are growing,
Their tiny buds are showing.
In summer it is hot,
We hike and swim a lot.
But autumn is the best,
Better than all the rest.
As the golden leaves are falling,
Before winter days come calling.

Timothy Atkinson (10)
Harmony Hill Primary School

Six Little Sticks On A Bramble Branch

Six little sticks on a bramble branch
Who resemble little horses on a western ranch.
Sweet, tiny insects, little acrobats
Playing in their homely tank,
Safe, away from cats.

Six little sticks with a bramble feast,
Munching to their hearts' content, happy to say the least.
Hungry little insects, tiny gymnasts
Living life to the full,
Never moving fast.

Six little sticks on a bramble branch,
Six little horses on my own little ranch.
Six stick insects, my best friends,
Playing games with them around
The fun never ends!

Kirsty McAuley (11)
Harmony Hill Primary School

Cats

C ool, crafty, crawling cats
A wake on their soft mats,
T ame tail twitching, I love my lovely cats,
S ome are black, some are white but best of all
   I like their sight.

Charlotte Matless (8)
Harmony Hill Primary School

ROAD TO NOWHERE

You're on a high, you passed your test,
You think you're quicker than the rest,
You're ready for a brilliant ride,
But you've a feeling deep inside.

Driving down a country lane,
Bad drivers really are a pain,
You wish you had paid more attention,
Rather than have a broken suspension.

You had a pint before your drive,
After it you may not be alive,
It's time to start wising up,
'Cause you're on the road to nowhere.

David Henry (11)
Harmony Hill Primary School

IN THE NIGHT

In the night,
everything dark.
In the night,
everything still.
In the night
I see my cat.
In the night
I see the moon
with its big white face.
It's dark as night,
dark as can be.
I can see some light,
so it must be the end of the night.

Alastair Toner (11)
Harmony Hill Primary School

GETTING THE HUMP

It certainly was
A weird experience
Starting off low
And ending up high,
When is it going to end?

With Mum and Dad in front
Holding on tight to little sis
As she was slipping off,
Jenna wasn't too happy
And I was following behind.

Hissing and biting,
Slipping and sliding,
Rocking from side to side
On my first camel ride.

Keith Hannigan (11)
Harmony Hill Primary School

CELEBRATION 2000

C elebrations are fun!
E veryone counts down the days
L ots of things are yet to be done
E laborate plans are being made
B ubbly drinks are put aside
R elations and friends are getting together
A nd all because the century ends.
T raditions of history are reflected upon
I nnovations for the future are being designed,
O n the stroke of midnight 1999
N ations will look forward to a new era of time.

Anthony Rough (8)
Harmony Hill Primary School

A Patchwork Quilt

Patchwork quilts, pink, blue or green,
Made up of tiny little pieces
That granny sews for me.
A pink square, a blue square
Or a diamond green as green.

Then sewn together on the noisy
Sewing machine with a sharp, silver needle.
My granny pushes the peddle with her foot,
The harder she pushes the faster it goes,
Once she let me have a go but I was too frightened.

After it's finished it's folded up
And my granny sells them to friends.
But this one is special,
It belongs to me,
Sitting beside me as lucky as could be!

Naomi Foster (9)
Harmony Hill Primary School

Celebration 2000

C entury almost over
E xcitment all around
L et's party
E njoy yourself
B egin a new millennium
R ace of time
A housework machine
T urn our calendar
E verybody having fun.

Sarah Mawhinney (8)
Harmony Hill Primary School

Dogs!

Dogs really are the most
Popular pets.
They are smarter than budgies
More loving than cats.

As friends they are in
A class of their own.
They can run and can play
And chew on a bone.

Dogs can be hairy, large,
Fat, thin or small.
One thing they all do is
Run after a ball.

They come in black, brown,
Golden or white
And some can be vicious
And give you a fright.

Most dogs are friendly and
Go for a run
And my German Shepherd Sabre
Is lots of fun.

Sabre loves being on the lead and
To go for a walk.
I just wish my friend Sabre
Could talk.

Andrew Stewart (9)
Harmony Hill Primary School

HORROR HOUSE

There is a house
At the top of the hill,
It's quite spooky
And it gives me a chill,
Its grass is too long,
It looks very scary,
They say there's a monster
And he's very, very hairy.

I'm afraid to go in
And to knock at the door
Just in case
I get pulled to the floor
By the big hairy guy.
It's my worst nightmare,
But my best friend
He just doesn't care.

He throws stones
At the windowpane,
The worst thing is
Is that he's insane,
He tries to break in
Through the front door,
He kicks it, hurts his foot
And falls to the floor.

A week went by,
I went back
Only to see it was fixed up.
People moved in,
I was amazed to see who,
It was my best friend!

Aaron Coulter (9)
Harmony Hill Primary School

WEEPING WILLOW

Weeping willow how sweet you are
Standing there as the day goes by,
Swaying to and fro in the whirling wind,
Standing patiently until spring.

Weeping willow in the spring,
Your buds should shoot out tenderly,
Watching the birds fly from the warm,
Gives you a happy, warm feeling in spring.

Weeping willow in the summer,
Watching the animals go by,
Enjoying the glorious sun in the day,
Having an enjoyable time.

Weeping willow in autumn,
Very sad indeed,
All your leaves are dying
And so are you.

Weeping willow in winter,
Oh so still and cold,
Don't despair the spring is coming,
New life for you I'm told.

Weeping willow how sweet you are
Standing there as the day goes by,
Swaying to and fro in the whirling wind,
Standing patiently until spring.

Leighanne Wright (10)
Harmony Hill Primary School

I SAW A MONSTER

I saw a monster lurking in the woods;
it got a bird and ate it, but then it really
started to regret it,
so it spat it out
and the bird leaped away.
The monster was huge
and it started stamping over me and gave
me a sore leg.

I ran away to my garden
and then it bit me and then I was
in his mouth, he spat me out
and then he stood on me and
I got squashed.

David Harkness (10)
Harmony Hill Primary School

WHEN I MOVED HOUSE

When I moved house it was hectic,
Boxes and bags everywhere.
You had to take care where you stepped,
Even when you sat down!

First we went to my gran's,
Then we went to the apartment,
Then we went over to my uncle's
And finally, we moved in!

I really miss my old house
And my old friends.
Oh why, oh why did we have to move
And start all over again?

Emma Gill (11)
Harmony Hill Primary School

FROM CHILDREN TO RATS

Four spiders' legs,
two rotten eggs.
Wax from an ear,
blood from a spear.
A dead mouse's tail
and a slimy, squashed snail.

Double, double,
toil and trouble,
fire burn and cauldron bubble.

Two pairs of smelly socks,
five old rusty locks.
A big toad's warts,
a vampire bat's wings,
two black ants
and lots of other things.

Double, double,
toil and trouble,
fire burn and cauldron bubble.

Mouldy old cheese,
blood from a pig,
heart of a deer
and an old man's wig.

Double, double,
toil and trouble,
fire burn and cauldron bubble.

This horrid spell
should mix very well!

Ashleigh McCoosh (10)
Harmony Hill Primary School

SPECIAL TIMES

We all celebrate special times,
Adults drink tasty wines.
Children eat popcorn and sweets
And even dance to groovy beats.

Listening to music in the candlelight,
People dancing underneath the spotlight.
Girls and guys at a table for two,
With flowers on their table, oh dear, achoo!

People parading down our street,
The big, big man playing a slow kind of beat.
People dancing all night long,
Up until the morning's break of dawn.

Lynsey Jess (10)
Harmony Hill Primary School

MY FIRST WORDS

My first word was ma,
My first word was da,
My mum was very happy
And so was my da.

My granny went all funny,
My granda went berserk,
They all said I was great
But I was a little late.

Most kids talk much earlier,
But to my mum I was still the best
And of course it didn't matter if I made a *mess!*

Nicola Henry (10)
Harmony Hill Primary School

Leaving

I am leaving my school this year
and I am very sad.
I have been here
for seven whole years.

I could go around this school
with my eyes shut tight.
I love this school better
than any other school.

I am in my last year in primary school
and I have to leave some of my friends
and go and make new friends
in grammar school.

I am excited about going
to grammar school
and having my own lockers
and meeting new friends.

Rebecca McCrossan (11)
Harmony Hill Primary School

The Vikings

The Vikings were fierce,
They didn't weep or plead,
They fought with determination,
Beating many a nation.

They were strong and bold,
Never to be beat,
They were known to plunder,
Just as strong as thunder.

They were not just soldiers,
But fishermen too,
You would never think
That their boats would sink.

As it struck midnight,
They became Christians,
They didn't raid much now,
But they still stayed tough.

Melissa Harris (10)
Harmony Hill Primary School

MOVING

The world is a box
with four cardboard sides.
'Mom where is my teddy?'
'In the box.'
'Mom where are my books?'
'In the box.'
Boxes, boxes, boxes.
'Mom I have only one shoe
what can I do?'
'Check the box.'
I can't leave my room because
I am scared that my bed
will be packed
up in a ?

Box!

Jenny Doherty (11)
Harmony Hill Primary School

SCHOOL'S OUT

School's out, school's out
Everybody shouts
Can't wait to get home
To get on the phone
To chat with my mates
And organise some groovy dates.

School's out, school's out
I'm glad to be out
No more reading books or stern leaders' looks
No more four four's are eight
No more longingly looking at the gate.

Schools out, schools out
Mum's wondering what it's all about
I'm on the phone with all my friends
There's lots for us to talk about
So here my story ends.

Ruth Thompson (11)
Harmony Hill Primary School

HALLOWE'EN

Hallowe'en so scary
Ah, the ghouls and ghosts.
Hallowe'en so fun
Oh, the treats for everyone.

I love when Hallowe'en comes round
With treats and fireworks to be found.
With ghost stories told by candlelight
Oh what fun we have on this hallowed night.

When we dunked for apples
There was water everywhere.
My mum said go to bed now
And I said that's not fair.

Craig Loney (9)
Harmony Hill Primary School

THE VIKINGS

Let's go back to the Dark Ages
Where fierce warriors called Vikings roamed around,
They were feared, for all the people who knew them,
Knew how they fought.

The Vikings' longboats were feared by some,
When they came to England, people watched in horror
As they sharpened their swords
And rushed off their ships with deafening war cries.

They came in their ships, raiding monasteries.
The Irish made a mistake letting them settle,
Realising all too quickly, Vikings didn't want peace,
They had to fight for their lives.

Hooray for King Alfred, if it wasn't for him
We would be worshipping Odin and Thor,
He built a navy and defeated them at sea
And drove the Vikings out.

I just can't get over what the Vikings were like,
Taking over countries without a fight,
Showing determination around the world,
Trading and invading was their game.

Alan Whitten (9)
Harmony Hill Primary School

AMAZING ANIMALS

Amazing animals far and near,
Amazing animals without fear,
In the jungle running like the wind,
Or in the rainforest enjoying the sun,
Amazing animals far and near,
Amazing animals without fear,
Tigers pounce, jump and roar, the wild cat chases the boar,
The colourful parrot soars through the air, the wind catching its
                                                                           colourful body,
The slithery snake slides through the grass hoping to find prey behind
                                                                           the next corner,
All these creatures are
Amazing animals far and near,
Amazing animals without fear.

Lauren Megaw (10)
Harmony Hill Primary School

CREEPY CATS

Black cats, creepy cats, crafty cunning, sleepy cats,
cats that are silly,
cats that are wise,
cats that steal and get a prize.

Moody cats, cunning cats,
cats that lie and purr,
ginger cats, tabby cats,
cats with fluffy fur.
Waiting for a dinner.

Ross Helsdon (9)
Harmony Hill Primary School

TITANIC

Been down there since 1912,
Nearly everything is hidden,
Just the old wrecked shell can be seen.
Now this is what I think happened.

It was a pleasure ship for first class people,
Not just as nice for third class,
Beautiful halls, beautiful dining rooms,
Now the terrible fate occurs.

The ship shakes, people scream,
Crew come down and shout,
'We are hit by an iceberg, everyone stay calm,'
But that did not calm the stirred.

Life jackets given out,
People flee to lifeboats,
The ship goes down and breaks in two,
100's of lives are lost.

Amy Porter (10)
Harmony Hill Primary School

COMBINE HARVESTERS

Combine harvesters are very loud,
Hear their engine roar like mad,
Beep the horn,
Cut the corn,
The grain goes into the trailer,
The tractor goes away,
Pours the grain out and
Roars away again.

Scott Matthews (10)
Harmony Hill Primary School

WHEN I WAS SMALL

When I was small
I used to crawl
onto the floor
and hit the door.
When I was small
I wanted to be a monkey,
I used to climb up trees,
I used to hang and swing.

When I was small
I had a friend who was a bully,
I had a friend who made a mess,
I had a friend who always said 'Yes'.
When I was small
I used to be a pain,
My sister was bigger than me,
She used to get the blame.

When I was small
My dad died,
I cried and cried and cried
The strongest tears of my life,
But you're always in my thoughts,
But someone else is in your place,
But at least I knew you
When I was small.

Lycette Harris (10)
Harmony Hill Primary School

MILLENNIUM

As you can see everything you used to know isn't as it seems:
The world is changing,
Who will see it first?
All stars so bright, glistening on that cold December night.
People ask and people wonder what will happen next?
They wait to celebrate.

Excited we all are, I know.
just a short matter of time to go.
Through the day and the night we stop to think . . .
The thought just makes me sink.
What will change? What will stay the same?

Before the sun the clock ticks twelve and darkness covers the world.
As darkness turns to light and sun rises at first sight
It is the dawn of a new era.
Millennium has risen.

Laura Rodgers (10)
Harmony Hill Primary School

THE MIND CHANGE

Eye of pig and granny's wig,
wax of ear and Budweiser beer,
one old mattress, one world atlas,
teacher's head (tastes good with bread),
Teletubbies' nose and a garden hose,
worms boil, *no not in the soil!*
One cat's tail and some brown ale,
and to finish off a pig's trough.

Patrick Stevenson (10)
Harmony Hill Primary School

IN THE YEAR 2000

The year 2000
Is a special year.
When the century turns
With balloons and wine
And everything fine,
We'll celebrate until 3am!

In the year 2000
Will everything change?
Will robots take over?
And will we use
Computers for everything?
(Even for school!)

In the year 2000
Will robots make
Things that will destroy us?
Destroy the human race?

Maybe I'm overdoing it,
Just a little bit.
I wonder what will happen
In the year 2000?

Nicola McGarel (9)
Harmony Hill Primary School

WINTER IS HERE

The wind was blowing through the trees,
The moon was very bright.
A little snowflake hit my cheek
And gave me a little fright.
A gust of wind hit the tree
And small icicles fell to the ground.

Water frozen on the ground,
Grass covered in dew,
Birds fly south to keep warm
And raindrops on your shoe
And that's how you know it's winter.

Jason Kerr (10)
Harmony Hill Primary School

AND THAT IS THAT

On my farm
The dog goes woof, woof,
The cow goes moo, moo,
The sheep goes baa, baa,
They eat,
They sleep
And that is that.

In my barn
The horse goes neigh, neigh,
The mouse goes nibble, nibble,
The owl goes tu-whit tu-whoo,
They eat,
They sleep
And that is that.

In my house
The baby cries,
My mummy moans,
My daddy groans,
They eat,
They sleep
And that is that.

Sarah Howes (10)
Harmony Hill Primary School

GROWN-UPS!

My mum says
'Timothy
are you watching me.'
'Yes.'
'Look at me when you talk.'
'Yes Mum.'
'How many times have
I told you.'
'A million times Mum.'

My dad says 'If you're
bored go out.'
'Can't.'
'There's no such word as can't.
Children today.'
'Yes Dad.'

My teacher says
'Are you listening?'
'Yes Miss.'
'You'll never learn anything if you don't.'
'Yes Miss.'
'Don't answer back.'
'Yes Miss.'
I don't listen
But I think a lot.

Shona Baldwin (10)
Harmony Hill Primary School

SWEETS THAT ROT YOUR TEETH

Sweets that rot your teeth
Are always so sweet.
You can pick from a number
Of different treats,
Some are very hard
And some are very soft,
But the only thing is they rot your teeth.

Sweets are so tasty
And nice to eat.
You can get them all colours,
That's why they're nice to eat.
Some sweets are horrible
And not nice to eat,
But the only thing is they still rot your teeth.

Mark Gribben (10)
Harmony Hill Primary School

MY FAMILY

First of all to start us off
My parents are very posh,
They wear big gowns
And always frown,
But you see my brother
Is a little bit of a clown,
My sister's a punk rocker
Which makes me sick!
She plays the guitar
And she's really, really wick!

I'm normal.

Michael Hunter (10)
Harmony Hill Primary School

The Moon

The moon is a big white balloon,
Sometimes it's a banana
Without any skin,
A ghost with only a head,
It's completely dead,
The moon.

Christopher Brady (10)
Harmony Hill Primary School

Rules

If I made the rules
I would protect the environment,
No more dumping chemicals,
No more toxic waste,
No more cutting trees down,
Let's make the world a better place.

If I made the rules
I would stop people fighting,
No more guns,
No more bombs,
No more nuclear wars,
Let's make the world a peaceful place.

If I made the rules
I'd make sure there was food for everyone,
No more starving people,
No more dirty water,
No more people dying,
Let's make the world a healthier place.

Christopher Boyd (10)
Killowen Primary School

THE BURGER

A burger is like a skyscraper . . .
You've got the ground floor a bun,
First floor, mayo dressing - going up,
Second floor, salad dressing - going up,
Third floor, delicious ketchup - going up,
Fourth floor, double bun,
Fifth floor, thousand island dressing - going up,
Sixth floor, beefburger plus onions - going up,
Seventh floor, hot brown sauce - going up,
Eighth floor, beefburger and melted cheese - going up,
Ninth floor, chopped onion - going up,
Top floor, sesame seed bun,
'There you are Sir,'
'Thank you,'
People call New York The Big Apple
But I call skyscrapers *burgers!*

Craig Hendley (10)
Killowen Primary School

SHARK

A thousand knives ready for the kill,
Its tongue serves the meal.
He books his table - a giant turtle's shell.
'Table for two,' he says, 'Me and my meal.'
For entertainment there's oysters and mussels
clapping to the beat of the instruments.
On his plate is a small, scrawny trout.
'That's only for starters!' cries the shark and
gobbles up the entire restaurant.
'Now,' he says with a grin, 'What's for dessert?'

Nicole Hill (10)
Killowen Primary School

A Sharpener

There's a monster that eats my pencils,
It devours them every day.

Its sharp teeth chew the wood up and throws the remains away.

Its favourite flavour is HB and it doesn't like the colour blue.

But it really, really loves red ones smothered in PVA glue.

This little monster might be tiny, but it's as ferocious as an angry bull.

You'd better watch out because its next meal could be you!

Natasha Wilson (10)
Killowen Primary School

In The Garden

In the garden I can see . . .
>green grass like a furry carpet,
>red roses like a blazing fire,
>daffodils like trumpets waiting to be played,
>trees with branches like long groping arms,
>a lawnmower that sounds like bumblebees,
>and looks like a squashed pram.

David Atchison (10)
Killowen Primary School

VIKING LONGSHIPS

Rowing hard against the tide
Our boat is swaying from side to side,
Across the ocean
To other lands,
Nobody can hide.
Going back and forth
To trade and raid,
Stealing precious jewels,
Going to foreign places,
Pitch our boats on the sands,
Going to find new lands,
To make our homes.
In bad weather the ocean foams.
Aching hands,
Selling slaves in other lands.
Raiding monasteries and churches,
Soon we'll be off on other searches.

Christopher Cowgill (10)
Killowen Primary School

DREAMING

Dreaming is like . . .
    sunbathing on a summer's day,
    floating down a river on a bed of silk,
    a drink of water in the desert's heat,
    diving in a crystal clear pool,
    a party that never ends,
    flying through fluffy clouds,
    or just drifting away on a pillow.

Daniel Agahi (10)
Killowen Primary School

VIKING LONGSHIPS

We're in the Viking longship
Ready for the daring trip,
Off we go,
We start quite slow,
Then we gather up some speed,
Pack the things that we'll need,
Ready for the raid,
Or is it maybe to trade?
We're ready for the raid,
Some of us are quite afraid,
We steal some gold,
Put it into the hold.
We got out alive,
Yes, we did survive!

Gary McCreery (10)
Killowen Primary School

RULES

If I made the rules I would make them fair,
There wouldn't be too many
So that people wouldn't care.
I would protect the Earth, the place where we stay,
Saving trees and hedges
And making safe places to play.

If I made the rules I would stop the lottery,
Because a lot of the time
It makes the winners unhappy,
Friends become jealous and families fight,
All because one of them
Got lucky one night.

If I made the rules there would be smaller classes,
There would be more work, but not masses and masses.
In my kind of school there would be less noise,
And girls would have fun
Without any boys!

Gillian Martin (10)
Killowen Primary School

INSIDE MY HEAD

There's a lot of things inside my head,
Things like 'What's for homework?'
Or 'What will I play today?'
'Will we move away
Or will we stay?'
'Will I finish my book today?'
There's scary things inside my head,
A great invention's hiding,
There's people inside my head
Working my eyes, nose, ears and mouth,
Giving me thoughts.
There's a camera taking pictures
So I don't forget things.
There's music . . .
And 'What will I wear tomorrow?'
There's a string of tables.
A lot of things inside my head,
I hope they don't get mixed up!

Lauren Wilson (10)
Killowen Primary School

DREAMING

Dreaming is like . . .
    going to Heaven,
    never using the number seven,
    jumping out of an aeroplane
    and floating all the way down
    to a place where there's no sound,
    gliding through the air,
    then meeting a big furry bear
    with lots of hair,
    like living in fairyland
    with miles of golden sand,
    like riding on a cloud
    and gently tumbling to the ground.

Dean McFall (10)
Killowen Primary School

DREAMING

Dreaming is like . . .
    a fairy tale filled with happiness that never ends,
    floating on a cloud shaped like a boat,
    climbing ice-cream mountains with
    rivers of chocolate sauce,
    a sparkling stream bursting with tropical fish,
    a gleaming sea filled with water babies,
    an air freshener that smells like a forest,
    a golden sea filled with silver sea horses
    that looks like a pond of melted gold.

Grace Morrison (10)
Killowen Primary School

Making A Difference

My babysitter I will pick,
She has always got a trick,
Her name is Hazel Haire
And she cleans everywhere.
She polishes windows and doors
And hoovers all the floors.
She picks up all my toys
But prefers girls to boys.
She never arrives late,
Nor forgets my birthday date.
She used to be quite tall
But now is getting small.
I have to admit she is quite old
But is worth her weight in gold.

Ryan Garvin (10)
Killowen Primary School

My First Day At School

Walking through the playground shaking,
There were no friends I was making,
People crowding round me, looking at my face,
Where was I?
What was this place?
A little girl asked,
'What's your name?'
'Don't know' I said, scared again.
The bell rang loudly in my ears,
Then started all my fears.

Chantelle Phillips (11)
Knockmore Primary School

MY FIRST DAY AT SCHOOL

I walked out through the front door
Thinking my mouth would hit the floor,
I jumped into the car
Steaming at full power,
I then walked through the school gate
Thinking would I find a mate,
I ran into the school
Thinking it was cool,
A little girl asked my name,
I was speechless,
Then the bell rang for home time.

Laura Moag (10)
Knockmore Primary School

MY FIRST DAY AT SCHOOL

On the first day of September
My mum drove me up.
When I got to the school gate
I hopped out of the car.
When I got into school
I started to cry,
Everyone started to look.
A girl called Stacey came over,
She asked me my name.
A bell went
It was home time.

Claire Armstrong (10)
Knockmore Primary School

MY FIRST DAY AT SCHOOL

I woke up early,
My mum dressed me,
She threw my pyjamas everywhere!
Where am I going?
She said nothing,
I got very scared,
She put my blouse on,
I broke the buttons on my blouse,
We arrived at a big house,
I thought it was a giant's house
(to begin with),
My mum called it a school,
A lot of children
Holding hands,
My mum said, 'Line up!'
I cried,
We went into a room,
I played with a lot of toys and children,
I had fun that day.

Leigh Pauley (10)
Knockmore Primary School

MR COOPER THE HEAD OF THE SCHOOL

Mr Cooper's not cool
But he's head of the school.
He makes a rule
And the rule's for the school.

When you break the rule
He shouts very loud.
And he makes you feel a fool
Which makes him very proud.

David Flanagan (10)
Knockmore Primary School

MILLENNIUM

As Robbie Williams says
Time is running out, there's
less than a year to go till the
year 2000. Computers are getting infected
with the 'Millennium Bug.' Is your computer
safe?
But there's also loads of things to celebrate,
on December 31st 1999 we'll get to party
the night away! With the millennium
not far away we won't be saying
'Happy New Year' instead it'll be
'Happy New Millennium!'
Eeh?

Emma White (11)
Moorfields Primary School

CELEBRATION

C is for celebrations
E is for excitement
L is for living for the millennium
E is for entertainment
B is for the Millennium Bug
R is for remembering the 90's
A is for amazement
T is for terrific fun
I is for injustice when the Bug strikes computers
O is for it being over
N is for the new year coming.

Gayle Armstrong (11)
Moorfields Primary School

CELEBRATING

Celebrating 2000 years which have gone by.
Celebrating the first light in the sky.
The first sound of a new baby's cry.
The satisfaction of granny's blueberry pie.
Celebrating everything man has made.
Even things as simple as a garden spade.
Things that we like, things that we don't.
Things that we do, things that we won't.
The year 2000 here it comes.
None of us can wait,
For when it comes, we'll all be there to,
Celebrate.

Brian Houston (11)
Moorfields Primary School

IT WAS ONLY A DREAM

Sitting on the bed is my rucksack,
My notebook and pen,
I'm wondering what to pack,
I've been at this since ten.

I have a hairbrush and matches
A sleeping bag and first aid kit
Markers and a notebook, a map and a compass
We are sure to need all of it.

We'll need warm clothes and boots,
Utensils, water and food.
A tent which we need to give roots
I hope it stays up, it should.

Ah, now we are going camping
I think this is so cool,
Hey what's that noise? *Riiinnnggg!*
Get up or you'll be late for school.

It was only a dream.

Alison Marks (10)
Moorfields Primary School

MILLENNIUM

Brand new year
With no fear
Of anyone
Or anything.

Brand new start
And apple tart,
Shaped like a heart,
Or fine art.

Brand new beginning,
I'm in the mood for winning
While the choir are singing,
I'll be starting a new beginning.

I'm in the mood for a new year,
I'm in the mood for a new start,
I'm in the mood for a new beginning,
Why, I'm definitely in a good mood.

Daena Carrie Lipsett (11)
Moorfields Primary School

WHAT DOES THE MILLENNIUM HOLD IN STORE?

The Millennium Bug is lurking,
In computers across the globe,
Waiting for the time to hatch,
It's awful masterplan.

All across the world,
Computers will freeze,
Lights will go off,
And documents will be lost.

Washing machines, cookers, VCRs and more,
Food will be lost,
Who knows what's in store?
All we know is there will be havoc galore.

So save your candles,
Print out files,
And make sure you prepare,
For the millennium war!

Frew Johnston (11)
Moorfields Primary School

The Millennium Dome

M is for the Millennium Dome,
I t is a very
L arge building,
L ively and weird.
E veryone will love it
N ot hate it.
N ear the River Thames
I t stands,
U nusual is the
M illennium Dome.

Pamela Livingstone (11)
Moorfields Primary School

Year 2000

Y es it's party time
E at and drink
A nd have real fun
R eady to party

2 much fun
0 it's great
0 it's fun
0 it's the best time ever.

Deborah Storey (11)
Moorfields Primary School

IN THE MILLENNIUM

I wonder if the price will go up
Or maybe down the chute?
I wonder if anything will change
Or maybe stay the same?

What will Sainsbury's be like
Will it get more ground?
What will the films be like in the cinemas
Will there be more horror around?

Will shopping be easier
Or will it be the same as always?
Will the money be all made of coin
Or will there still be some paper money?

I read about floating cars
Like the one on the Jetsons
I read about a Millennium Bug
That might break computers.

On TV I saw a shopping scanner
You only have to push your trolley through.
I also saw a frog
With a yellow chest.

I wonder what the shoes will be like
Will they be weird
Will they look short
Or will they have long heels?

I hope the millennium
Will be a lot different
Than it is at the moment
And be a lot more fun.

Selina Shingleton (11)
Moorfields Primary School

Brown

That thick tree trunk I can climb.
The beautiful shimmering of the horse's mane.
The ground that we sow and harvest.
The old dam, dirty with pollution.
An eagle soaring high.

James Spence (9)
Mossley Primary School

White

The thin wispy clouds in the morning sky
The thick wool of sheep caught on the fence
The glint of sun on the window
A big shiny balloon at a party
Guilty in court.

Darryl McConnell (9)
Mossley Primary School

Green

Thundering crocodiles snapping everywhere.
Poisonous ivy creeping up tall plants.
Beautiful tasty apples hanging down from trees.
Evil monsters scaring everyone.
Precious emeralds sparkling in the sun.

Michael Mahon (9)
Mossley Primary School

FEARS

I feel afraid when I see a snake,
And when I hear a strange noise,
And if I'm alone I am scared.
My biggest fear is being stuck in a lift,
And going on a ghost train.
When I am scared I fight my fears,
Or I tell my mum or even hide,
And then I feel much better.

Jonathan Acheson (9)
Mossley Primary School

BLUE

Bright sugar paper to back my book.
The dark deep angry sea, roaring.
Pale cloudless sky.
Cold frosty mornings on my way to school.
Fields of flax are blowing in the wind.

Sarah Lynas (9)
Mossley Primary School

RED

The blood pumps in my body
The volcano erupts in the mountains
I feel cosy in bed
Anger in many people's faces
My mum's new skirt.

Gary Johnston (9)
Mossley Primary School

A Creation Poem

C reation,
R ainbow colours in the skies.
E agles that soar through the sky.
A nts which crawl about.
T arantulas that move all about,
I nsects that are very slimy.
O ceans for ships to sail on,
N ations for people to live on.

Dale Huston (9)
Mossley Primary School

Humpty Dumpty

Humpty Dumpty went to the park
Humpty Dumpty was afraid of the dark
He walked and walked
And walked a bit more
And Humpty Dumpty began to snore.

Matthew Boyd (9)
Mossley Primary School

Black

An evil silence that covers the earth.
The dark blackness nobody can see through.
A thick mist, rising from the mountains.
Everybody goes in, when night touches the sky.

Andrew Innes (9)
Mossley Primary School

SOUNDS BEHIND THE DOOR

doors creaking
taps dripping
toasters popping
TVs blaring
telephones ringing
toilets flushing
microwaves droning
pianos tinkling
brothers crying
sisters shouting
plates breaking
clocks ticking
dryers rumbling
kettles whistling
doorbells ringing
violins screeching.

Sarah Knight (9)
Mossley Primary School

CREATION

C reation.
R hinos are running.
E agles are flying.
A pples in the orchard.
T rees are getting chopped down.
I ndians are running around the fire.
O ctopuses are swimming in the ocean.
N ature's animals are brilliant!

Matthew McCracken (9)
Mossley Primary School

SOUNDS BEHIND THE DOOR

Alarm clocks ringing
Windows smashing
Cats miaowing
Toilets flushing
Dads making earthquakes up the stairs
Women on phone
So enjoying,
Sausages sizzling in the pan
Forks clattering
Knives as well
Sausages crunching in my mouth,
Going to bed
Hear my snoring.

Graeme Adam Fitzsimmons (9)
Mossley Primary School

HAPPINESS IS . . .

Happiness is watching the World Cup
It is great.
Happiness is when Rangers score
And I love them.
Happiness is when they score
Feeling great
Eating fish and chips
Knowing they will win.
Happiness is when they score
And watching the World Cup.

Karl Cosgrove (9)
Mossley Primary School

SOUNDS BEHIND THE DOOR

Dogs barking
Cats miaowing.
Mice squeaking.
Taps dripping.
Toilets flushing.
Birds singing.
Children screaming.
Sausages sizzling.
Glasses breaking.
Toasters popping.
Music blasting.
Telephones ringing.
Pianos playing.
TVs blaring.
Clocks ticking.
Microwaves pinging.
Kettles whistling.
The day is over.

Daniel Watson (9)
Mossley Primary School

FEARS

I feel afraid when I am doing a test.
And when I am in the toilet.
And if I'm on my own in the forest.
My biggest fear is heights.
And guns.
When I'm scared I stay calm.
Or I run or even squeal.
And then I feel fine.

Gary Couser (9)
Mossley Primary School

HAPPINESS IS . . .

Happiness is riding my bike
It is opening my presents on my birthday.
Happiness is the atmosphere at my birthday
And the atmosphere of Christmas too.
Happiness is Christmas
Feeling of holidays
Eating and drinking, pizza and chocolate
Knowing it's my birthday.
Happiness is knowing my mum loves me
And playing tennis.

Rebecca Davidson (9)
Mossley Primary School

HAPPINESS IS . . .

Happiness is puppies chasing their tails.
It's nice to go to Jungle Jims
Happiness is warm by the fire
And going swimming in a pool.
Happiness is making snowmen.
Feeling puppies licking your hands.
Eating big Whoppers at Burger King
Knowing things are ok.
Happiness is finding ladybugs and butterflies.

Mark Fenning (9)
Mossley Primary School

SOUNDS BEHIND THE DOOR

Windows b r e a k i n g
Toilets flushing
Cats miaowing
Big dogs barking
Fat sizzling
Doors banging
Water d
　　　r
　　　i
　　　p
　　　p
　　　　i
　　　　　n
　　　　　　g
Phones bleeping
Microwaves humming
Tumble driers rumbling
Tummies squirming
Plates s m a s h i n g
Televisions blaring
Clocks ticking.

Benjamin Thomas Davis (9)
Mossley Primary School

BICYCLE

Dark blue
Very fast bike
Ringing my loud bell
Smashing!

Matthew Wilson (8)
Mossley Primary School

HAPPINESS IS . . .

Happiness is baking with my granny.
It is having a water fight in the summer.
Happiness is getting presents on my birthday
And playing with my cousin.
Happiness is going to a party
Feeling happy with my mum and dad.
Eating toasted marshmallows by the fire.
Knowing I'm going to have a midnight feast soon.
Happiness is going swimming
And playing with my kitten.

Victoria Braden (9)
Mossley Primary School

EASTER

E aster Sunday coming
A nd our Easter holidays are near
S un shining down
T reats for the family
E xcitement for children
R eally it's an exciting day.

Adam Anderson (9)
Mossley Primary School

RAIN

Bucketing down
Real heavy gushes
Watching water drum hard
Nuisance.

Jonathan Lowans (8)
Mossley Primary School

SOUNDS BEHIND THE DOOR

Girls screaming
Whistles whistling
Sausages sizzling
Doors slamming
Chimes tinkling
Toilets flushing
Pianos playing
Dogs barking
Cats purring
Adam crying
Mark singing
Popcorn popping
Glass smashing
Cars crashing
Water splashing
Mice squeaking
Daddy snoring
Quiet!

Steven Davidson (8)
Mossley Primary School

CREATION

C reation.
R obins flying in the sky.
E lephants in Belfast Zoo.
A lligator in a swamp.
T urkey at Christmastime.
I gloos in Iceland.
O ctopuses in the sea.
N ature in my garden.

Lesley Ann Hoey (9)
Mossley Primary School

BEDROOM FOR RENT

Bedroom for rent,
No room to breathe.
One pretty clock,
Never right
Gives an excuse for being late.
Bed is used for a trampoline
And for sleeping in.
Built-in wardrobe, full of clothes.
Please knock, signs, don't work.
Carpets and curtains lovely,
No reasonable offer refused.

Fiona Young (8)
Mossley Primary School

BEDROOM FOR RENT

Bedroom for rent
Brilliant!
Windows small,
Wardrobe turned to side makes good hut.
String off light, makes good Action Man swing
Loads of fun.
Carpet nice, slidey and comfortable.
Brother as slave.
Sister does cleaning.
Lots of pillows for bed.
No reasonable offer refused.

Darren Taylor (9)
Mossley Primary School

EASTER

E aster eggs made of chocolate.
A ll children have fun.
S mall chicks come out from speckled eggs on Easter Sunday.
T o see their mother.
E aster bunnies have fun.
R eady for school concert, I just can't wait.

Hyunchul Yang (9)
Mossley Primary School

EASTER

E aster holidays
A t the school concert
S weet daffodils blowing in the breeze
T he lambs skipping about
E aster chicks hatching
R abbits playing happily in the fields.

Danielle Earley (9)
Mossley Primary School

BICYCLE

Amazing speed.
Supersonic stunts.
Look how fast I go.
Fantastic!

Stephen Monaghan (9)
Mossley Primary School

THE STRANGER

The rain pelting down
Was making me feel terrified.
Last quarter of the moon was showing.
Frosty cold all around me.
There stood a creature face to face with me.
My legs turned to jelly.
He cackled.
Smoke billowed from his mouth.
I was astonished.
His luminous body glowed blue, green and yellow.
It dazzled me.
He gurgled and warbled loudly.
I was shocked.
He moved towards me.
Am I dreaming?
He shot gas towards me,
In a puff of smoke he was gone.
I lay in the wet grass,
Stunned.

Simon McMullan (8)
Mossley Primary School

HUMPTY DUMPTY

Humpty Dumpty went to the moon
Humpty Dumpty went on a spoon.
He brought some apples
And a tent
But when he landed, the spoon got bent.

Noel Beckett (9)
Mossley Primary School

HUMPTY DUMPTY

Humpty Dumpty went for a swim
Humpty Dumpty got so thin
He saw a big ship
Which came quite close
The ship got covered in Humpty's yolk.

Phillip Sloan (9)
Mossley Primary School

HUMPTY DUMPTY

Humpty Dumpty went to the moon
Humpty Dumpty sat on a spoon.
He found an alien
When he got there
An ugly creature with bright green hair.

Andrew Nicholl (8)
Mossley Primary School

HUMPTY DUMPTY

Humpty Dumpty went to school
Humpty Dumpty looked very cool
He didn't listen
He was bad at sums
And he didn't have any fun with his chums.

Cassie Clair Arkins (9)
Mossley Primary School

THE STRANGER

The stars and moon were shining brightly in the blackness of the sky.
There stood a monster face to face with me.
My heart pounded fast,
When blazing rays came from his huge green eyes.
I was horrified.
He gave me a hard stare.
He bellowed at me.
I was terrified.
I squealed,
As huge balls of gas shot towards me.
I fell onto the wet grass.
He gave me a menacing look.
Then he disappeared.

Amy Cooke (9)
Mossley Primary School

FEARS

I feel afraid when I see snakes
And when I see a spider.
And if I'm scared I will run to my mum.
My biggest fear is when there's a spider, a hairy spider
And it's in the bog and I close my eyes.
When I'm scared I cry and run out the back door
Or I chase it out of the room
Or I cry or even say something
And I feel better.

Claudia Ashe (9)
Mossley Primary School

THE STRANGER

The frost glistens
The silver moon is full
It's freezing outside
There stood a creature face to face with me!
My mouth opened
But I couldn't scream.
Smoke came from his belly button
I was horrified.
The creature blinked his six eyes,
Then glared at me.
A low quiet belching came from his mouth.
I was confused.
A star hit my forehead.
Then I really did scream.
The creature disappeared in a puff of aquamarine smoke,
As I ran off home again.

Rebekah Fenning (8)
Mossley Primary School

BEDROOM FOR RENT

Bedroom for rent
A little poky but,
Cosy and bright.
At the top of the stairs
Walls with paintings (mice included).
Gutters on the outside for climbing.
Comes with free package - your mum!
Junk pile - your very own Ben Nevis.

Daniel Barnett (8)
Mossley Primary School

BEDROOM FOR RENT

Bedroom for rent,
Bright purple curtains to swing on,
Welcoming spiders,
Multicoloured wallpaper to strip.
Lovely dirty windows to peer through,
Stars hanging from the ceiling,
Two cockatiels to keep you awake.
Brilliant books, torn apart,
And the extra gift, Mum.

Rebecca Edgar (9)
Mossley Primary School

GOLDFISH

Swimming around with nothing to do,
A castle to play with,
A window to look through.

It seems so easy just gliding along,
I whistle with glee,
As I swim all day long.

A cat comes along,
Dips his paw in the tank,
He didn't catch me 'cause I hid at the back.

Swimming around with nothing to do,
I just play all day,
What a life for me and you.

Clare Wallace (11)
Oakfield Primary School

SAM

He's always wriggling about the house,
He often likes a nice fat mouse
Some people think he feels slimy,
And others see him and go . . . blimey!
As soon as I wake up I hear the hiss
But I can't help it; I give him a kiss.

Mum always chases him with a broom,
Whenever he slithers into her room
In the autumn he sheds his skin,
Mum makes me throw it in the bin
My friends think that because I have a *snake* I'm mad
But Sam's just like me, always good and never bad!

Brian Irvine (10)
Oakfield Primary School

DOWN BY THE SEASHORE

Down by the seashore,
Where the seashells lay,
There was a small sea-snail
Who slowly slithered away.

He left a silver trail behind him,
Which glistened in the moon.
I hope I see another one
Slither along soon.

Claire Crawford (11)
Oakfield Primary School

THE BROWN DOG

The brown dog sits,
As quiet as a mouse,
Keeping a watch,
Over the house.

She stands on all four,
When she hears a noise,
And goes to the door,
To see only some boys.

She shows her sharp teeth,
And lets out a bark,
Then suddenly the boys,
Run to the park.

Walking back in,
Proud as can be,
She goes to sleep,
On her master's knee.

Claire Auld (11)
Oakfield Primary School

THE RAINBOW

Whenever there's a shower of rain,
Everyone is sad,
But then out comes the sunshine,
And everyone is glad.

Because a rainbow has appeared,
Before their very eyes,
To put a smile upon their face,
And brighten up the skies.

With colours from the brightest green,
To indigo so bold,
And if you reach the end of it,
You might find a pot of *gold!*

Rhonda Humphreys (11)
Oakfield Primary School

THE MARS VOLCANO

And now my friends, lend me your ears,
And listen to my tale.
The year was 2099,
And in the town of Krail,

On Mars, Olympus Mons was lurking,
The tallest volcano ever!
The scientists pronounced him dead,
And thought themselves quite clever.

'Extinct? Me?' he rumbled,
With an almighty roar.
'I'll give them extinct, indeed!
Then Krail will be no more!'

The Martians heard a rumble,
But it was far too late!
The lava rushed to meet them,
And sealed their dreadful fate.

So that, my friends, was my tale,
My chronicle, my story.
And next time I spin you a yarn,
It won't be quite so gory.

Susan Jones (11)
Oakfield Primary School

THE LEMMING

The lemming has fur which is light,
But sadly it's not very bright.
It's not very tall,
And its brain is small,
It throws itself from a huge height.

Christopher Johnston (11)
Oakfield Primary School

CELEBRATION 2000

Everybody will be out on the street
You never know who you will meet
Laughing, joking, having fun
The party will run and run
Food, drinks, cakes and buns
And lots of prizes to be won.
I am dreading the Millennium Bug,
It will eat through computers just like a drug.

I can't wait until Big Ben strikes 12.00
And then the party will really go
People will be dancing
And horses will be prancing,
Lots of different treats
And lots of different kinds of things to eat
Now I will leave you to enjoy the fun.

Richard McMillan (10)
Parkgate Primary School

CELEBRATION 2000

The new millennium is coming
How do we celebrate
Everybody's dancing and singing in the street.

Now we need fireworks to light up the beautiful sky at night.
Even we're getting so excited
We will celebrate with our friends and families.

M aybe I will not die
I   might live to be 400
L eaves might never fall or change colour.
L ively music rings in my ears.
E ven in the morning
N ow we're getting closer
I   just can't wait
U niversal movies will change in the new
M illennium.

Ryan Irvine (10)
Parkgate Primary School

CELEBRATION 2000

I like to party,
I like to dance,
I like to scream,
I like to sing,
I want to be a DJ,
It will be fun,
I'll dance all night,
I'll listen to music,
I love celebration so,
I'll party for the millennium.

Simon McClay (9)
Parkgate Primary School

CELEBRATION 2000

C hristmas will be exciting
E verybody is celebrating the New Year
L ooking forward to the millennium
E veryone is getting excited, having
B rilliant parties which
R un on through the night,
A mazing fireworks will go off
T ables of food and drink
I can't wait until the millennium
O n that night, I'll stay up until dawn
N obody will miss the millennium.

Daniel McMillan (9)
Parkgate Primary School

CELEBRATION 2000

C ome to the party
E veryone is going to be there.
L ooking at the happy faces.
E nemies are becoming friends.
B anging, exploding fireworks.
R ekindling friendships has begun.
A rrangements are being made.
T rouble is no more.
I mprovements have come.
O utstanding monuments have been built.
N ever again will I be part of this huge celebration.

Adam McClay (10)
Parkgate Primary School

HAPPY CELEBRATION

C elebrations will be all over the streets
E xciting things will happen non stop.
L isten to the cheers when it reaches 12 o'clock
E ven the cats will miaow
B arking dogs will howl
R unning round the streets, that's where I will be
A bout to strike twelve.
T he fireworks are ready to explode and sparkle
I 'm thinking about what is going to happen
O n the first day of the year 2000
N ever will we forget this night.

Lisa McCartney (9)
Parkgate Primary School

WHAT A MILLENNIUM

C elebration 2000 will be the best.
E veryone will join in with the party feast.
L oved the past 1000 years and now we say goodbye.
E veryone will celebrate out in the streets.
B eer cracked open,
R aves, parties, dancing, fireworks and madness.
A night which we will never forget.
T ummies will be trembling waiting for
BI g Ben to strike.
O verall this will be the best night of our lives.
N ow we are starting a new millennium.

Kelly Ann Connor (10)
Parkgate Primary School

NEW YEAR'S EVE '99

More than cold in the air
Icicles hang but I don't care
Lots of parties on the street
Load of people that you meet
When the fireworks are alight
I just hope they're really bright
On the first New Year's Day
I will go on out to play
Then I'll have a snowball fight
Oh that was a brilliant sight
Everyone happy, laughing and gay
That's because it's the very first day
Of a new millennium.

Sarah Cuthbertson (9)
Parkgate Primary School

CELEBRATION 2000

A new millennium comes to us
And brings us lots of fuss.
New jobs there will be.
Perhaps one for me and
I hope that I am well and fit
To see the fireworks being lit.
On New Year's Day
I'll go and play
And have a snowball fight.
I think that I,
Should have a try
At starting a brand-new life.

Natasha Henderson (8)
Parkgate Primary School

A MILLENNIUM RIDDLE

I live inside computers, TVs and all machines,
I eat my way through wires
I have fried batteries for tea.
All I need's electric,
And I'm happy as can be
Have you guessed who I am?
I'm the Millennium Bug you see.

People say they'll party from dusk,
Right on till dawn.
But when they come into their house,
Their computers will be gone
Aeroplanes will drop down
Everyone will drown.
So I shall be the only thing that parties on till dawn.

Jamie McMillan (10)
Parkgate Primary School

WE'RE THE COMPUTER KIDS

We don't need teachers anymore -
They are such an awful bore.
With computers nowadays
We can learn in different ways -
Compose a story, type and print,
Send e-mails and receive those sent,
Surf the internet, find out information,
Solve difficult mathematical calculations.
So we're the computer kids and we're here to stay,
So I think we should sack the teachers straight away.

Louise Adair (11)
Rathenraw Integrated Primary School

TIGER MIGHT

Tiger, tiger of the night,
Your stripes are dark, but your coat is bright.
You snap your jaws in the night.
When people shoot at you, you run with fright.
You run through the forest with all your might.

Your muscles are strong,
Your teeth are sharp and your tail is long.
Go and hide in the darkness of the night.

Fighting with a zebra would be quite tough
Fighting with a lion would be really rough.
They would pull you to the ground
But I know you are very strong.
You'd say, 'You're not beating me.'
For your teeth are sharp like a set of knives
So other animals beware of your lives!

Michael Knox (10)
Rathenraw Integrated Primary School

DREAMING

I was sitting in class writing in my book.
The sun was out.
I thought about a shooting star.
A comet was heading for the world.
The moon was up.
I felt I was sitting on another planet or galaxy.
There were sponges that were squishy.
I saw an alien which smelled like cheese and tomato.
Oh I must stop dreaming and get on with my writing.

Christopher McClelland (9)
Rathenraw Integrated Primary School

ICE

When I lift the ice it is blisteringly bright,
My fingers burn with the cold.
The ice melts like fizz in the bright light.
It crackles like a feather so bright and soft.
The sun goes in and out,
It goes in and out.
Then the ice cries goodbye
Before it melts away.
Its family cry one last tear goodbye.
Everyone knows ice can't stay forever.

Sarah El-Hamalawy (8)
Rathenraw Integrated Primary School

THE MOON

The moon is a beautiful thing.
It is yellow and glittery and bright
Like a beautiful singer in jeans.
It is sparkly - like a friend of the stars.
It is as hot as fire.
It lives in space, in the dark
Aliens are its enemies.
Every time you walk at night it follows you -
I wonder why it does that.

Martina Reed (9)
Rathenraw Integrated Primary School

SPACE

The world is big and round.
The moon is bright,
It's golden,
High up in the sky,
Far away from the Earth.
The sun is nearer the Earth.
The stars are far away from the Earth too.

David McClelland (9)
Rathenraw Integrated Primary School

TIGER, TIGER

Tiger, tiger in the night, burning very bright.
Fierce as a lion,
Big as a leopard.
He'll kill you dead as quick as a flash,
With those big black claws and those big orange feet.
I'll not be visiting him at night.

Robert Smith (9)
Rathenraw Integrated Primary School

THE BATH

The bath is slippy with bubbles,
The bubbles sparkle like the stars.
The bath water is very warm,
The bubbles froth on top.
I pretend to swim in the bath -
Swimming down, deep deep into the ocean!

Mairead Gribbon (9)
Rathenraw Integrated Primary School

POPSTARS

When they walk on the stage
The sparkled lights go on,
They dance to the loud music
The stage is like glitter,
The popstars are so famous
People sit and watch and twinkle their eyes,
The popstars are amazed!

Victoria Patty (9)
Rathenraw Integrated Primary School

I HEAR THE WIND

The wind whispers,
Howls down my chimney
Whispers in my ear
All
   is
      quiet.

Steven Jones (9)
Rathenraw Integrated Primary School

LISTENING

A gentle breeze
      blowing.
Then a lion roaring.
Moaning and groaning.
Softly blowing
Whispers
      Quiet.

Graeme Clarke (9)
Rathenraw Integrated Primary School

My Friend

Conor is a special friend,
Who stays with me to the end.
He will tell a few jokes if he likes.

He's kind and gentle and never fights.
He is never rude and disgusting,
He is very quiet and humorous.
We have a special friendship,
Which no one can undo.

John Mulholland (10)
Rathenraw Integrated Primary School

Break Time

I stroll over to my favourite spot in the playground,
The wall beside the bushes.
Glancing at the sky
A clear ocean greets me.
I stand on its reflection.
My head rotates,
The grass twinkles in my eye,
A bed for fairies.
A rainbow of colours shoot past me
Trying to keep warm.
My name echoes around the playground
I awaken from my trance.

Natalie Smyth (11)
St Catherine's Primary School, Belfast

A FROSTY MORNING

I stand in a carpet of soft white wool,
The bitter wind blows through my body,
I cuddle, cradle, comfort myself.
The glittering clouds float away,
A large grey rat hovers over me,
I want to run and hide.
Steam comes out of my mouth,
Children run past me, pushing another gust of wind my way,
I shake and shiver.
My face is a block of ice,
I long to escape this torture.

Sadhbh Smyth (11)
St Catherine's Primary School, Belfast

BREAK TIME

Children run wildly up and down
A pale sparkling white blanket.
A biting, boreal monster
Is chasing them.
They are shivering, shaking screaming
Trying to escape from his cold breath.

Puffy pillows of clouds
Suddenly burst with snow
Camouflaging the world below.
Children's gobsmacked faces
Show their joy.

Deirdre Bowman (10)
St Catherine's Primary School, Belfast

THE RAINFOREST

Down on the gloomy forest floor
Lie the mice, crawling about to catch flies.
Crunch, crunch, crunch, the sound of the trodden leaves.
The deer comes running swiftly in.
Nowhere to go, nowhere to hide.
His dark tanned coat
Matches the old wrinkled barks of the trees.
He's getting closer.
I'll jump into this bush hoping he'll go.
I can come out now, calm and relaxed.

Margaret Sarah Mooney (11)
St Catherine's Primary School, Belfast

THE RAINFOREST

I stand alone looking at the colourful birds.
Fruit and leaves fall down.
Leaves are coloured green, orange, red.
Hot weather makes you feel like putting yourself in a fridge or freezer.
Caterpillars, camouflaged, lying on a leaf.
Birds whistle continuously.
I leave this part of the rainforest,
Missing it already.

Roisin Flynn (11)
St Catherine's Primary School, Belfast

My Granny

My granny's hair is as white as snow
There is a reason she's ninety-two you know.
She sits at the fire and tells stories of saints,
Mostly of Jesus and how kind he was.
She gives me candles to light at night
And prayers to say at daylight.
She wears gold glasses
And always wears a shawl,
She makes me laugh when I am sad
And hugs me when I fall.
My granny is the best of them all.

Caron Donnelly
St Catherine's Primary School, Belfast

A Day In January

I stand in the playground clutching my hands
My cheeks are rosy red
Stained with the mark of the frost
Children stand in huddles trying to keep warm.
Ice on the ground makes some slip.
Trees are waving, swaying in the harsh wind
Blown about like paper bags
Leaves are zooming like helicopters.
My hair stands on end
I am being electrocuted.

Lisa Cosgrove (10)
St Catherine's Primary School, Belfast

BREAK TIME

As I stand in our playground,
I huddle together with my friends,
I shiver as the frosty monster
Wraps around me.
I glance down,
I see a glittery, glacial, wizard's cloak
Covering the ground.
Peering upwards at the puffy cotton wool sky,
I wish the bell would ring,
So I can escape the cold.

Isabelle McHenry (10)
St Catherine's Primary School, Belfast

ME-TAPHOR!

I am Belfast City busy and noisy,
Filled with shops with amazing things,
I am a small furry tabby cat sometimes shy,
Purring and miaowing contentedly,
I am a comfortable bed, warm and dreamy,
Keeping you warm in wintertime,
I am summer hot and sunny,
Everyone around is having fun,
I am a wedding, a time of joy and happiness,
Dancing and singing for hours on end,
I am a sweet puppy dog, cute and exciting
Always there when someone needs me,
I am the golden sun, lighting up your life,
Bright, hot and gigantic,
I am a comet blazing with excitement
Usually the centre of attention.

Siobhan Crummey (10)
St Colman's Primary School, Lambeg

ME AND MY AMAZING LIFE

I am a forest so friendly with nature
I shade the flowers that grow in spring
I am yellow so bright and cheerful
Giving happiness and brightness to you
I am a kiwi so smooth and hairy
Bringing nutrients to your body
I am a parrot always talking
My noise will burst your eardrums
I am a trumpet with a noisy expression
Giving songs nice tunes
I am autumn leaves falling
Ripping the skin off trees
I am a football always scoring
Putting happiness into football fans.

Ciaron Flannery (9)
St Colman's Primary School, Lambeg

MATERIALS

Cotton is my name
Making clothes is my game
You can make shirts out of me
Lots of colours for all to see

I grow in fields
I'm picked and washed
And then I'm stretched
And rolled into a batch.

Deborah Kearney (9)
St Colman's Primary School, Lambeg

THINK OF ME

I am a red leaf fluttering in the wind,
If you tried to rip me you wouldn't be able to,
I am a blue and wet drop of rain falling from the sky,
When I hit the ground I splash into small droplets,
I am a red juicy and sweet strawberry,
When you bite me you won't ever be hungry again,
I am a fluffy Christmas stocking full of presents,
You can put a whole toy store in me,
I am a jungle full of animals and plants,
They are all energetic and beautiful,
I am a yellow, furry and tiny hamster running in my wheel,
I never get tired of running in it,
I am a round, white and bouncy football,
When you kick me I'll always go into the net,
I am a book about adventure that never ends,
The pictures in me are 4D and very exciting,
I am a sword that can cut through metal, wood, paper and glass,
I will never go blunt and I will always stay shiny.

Brendan Wright (10)
St Colman's Primary School, Lambeg

THE BATTLE

The longships crunch onto the shore
And the Vikings all spill out,
Yelling and crying wildly
As they run about.

The cold waves crash
And the north wind howls,
As the cruel battle begins
With savage screams so loud.

Setting fire to houses,
Killing anyone in their way,
In the life of a warrior
This is another glorious day.

Kathryn McCann (9)
St Colman's Primary School, Lambeg

MY BEST FRIEND IS . . .

She is the sun rising
Behind the rainy clouds.
In the freezing weather
She is the stony ground.

She is an old rattly bed
In the corner of a room.
She is a lion padding slowly
Through the mountain gloom.

She is the rain falling softly
Down through the cold blue sky.
She is the white ball on the pool table
Clicking off the others when you play.

She is the one and only red rose
On the dark thorn bush.
She is a jingling pinball machine
That you push and push and push.

Who is she?

Claire Kennedy (10)
St Colman's Primary School, Lambeg

My Mum

She is a sunny afternoon
in the heart of America.
In the corner of a room
she is an old rocking chair.
She is a rabbit
jumping about in the grass.
She is a rainbow after a shower,
all the colours clash.
She is a beautiful yellow sunflower,
her petals soft and bright.
She is a wonderful washing machine
that makes our clothes white.

Seanin Sands (9)
St Colman's Primary School, Lambeg

Viking

Crash go the waves
On to the sandy beach
Crack go the shells
As heavy feet crush
Splinter them to bits
Swish goes the axe
As it swings towards the tree

Crunch go the leaves
As we creep through the night-time town
And then with booming cries
We attack!

James Ferguson (10)
St Colman's Primary School, Lambeg

ME: INSIDE MY HEAD

I am a mysterious jungle, wild and adventurous
Full of dangerous things.
I am gold, rare and expensive
Shining with brightness.
I am a tiny grape, small but bursting with flavour,
A tiny bunch of goodness.
I am a purring, ginger tabby cat, warm and gentle
Quietly creeping around the house.
I am in the dark roller-coaster, full of fun and excitement
Never knowing what's going to happen next.
I am a big armchair, very comfortable and warm.
Always there when you need it.
I am Christmas Eve, full of happiness and excitement,
White snow softly landing outside.

Tara Watterson (9)
St Colman's Primary School, Lambeg

CRAZY HORSE

He stands down there at the side of the wall
Looks like he's going to fall
He drinks and drinks like a lunatic
Always looks like he's really sick
His ugly smile scared me today
Sometimes I wish he'd just go away
He sleeps in the street, not in a bed
He has no pillow for his head
He's so thin you can see his bones
His eyes are black, whirling stones.

Bridgeen Conlon (10)
St Colman's Primary School, Lambeg

ME

I am a Celtic superstore, always green and white,
Always selling things people want
I am a yellow banana, juicy and erupting with goodness,
I taste nice and never go out of date.
I am a trumpet always loud,
To make myself heard,
Always clean and shining like a knight in armour.
I am a furious lion, active at sports always,
I can catch my prey no problem.
I am a comfortable armchair never breaking down
When someone big sits on me.
I am the sunshine full of good things,
Never letting rain take over,
I never let the children down in summer.

Cormac McCloskey (10)
St Colman's Primary School, Lambeg

ME

I am a burger stand sizzling and juicy and hot

I am a red apple shining with ripeness

I am an orange bursting with sparkle
Jumping with fear to see if he was eaten

I am a tiger hungry with anger fearlessly killing

I am a cello out of tune breaking the silence
of the night.

Carl Adams (10)
St Colman's Primary School, Lambeg

ME

I am a beach warm and dry with a high tide
I crash onto the sand with big strong waves.
I am a shade of glooming bright green
I glow in the dark like a bright light.
I am a pineapple juicy and sharp, ready to be eaten
by a starving person.
I am a lion ready to pounce on its quick and stubborn prey.
I am a cello deep and mysterious and ready to be played on
by a musician.
I am a volcano ready to create an earthquake then explode
and pour out all my lava.
I am an eagle ready to swoop on my prey and grab it
by the neck and eat it.

Conor O'Reilly (9)
St Colman's Primary School, Lambeg

IMAGES OF ME

I am a great white shark hungrily awaiting a victim.
I rip and tear at tender legs and hairy arms.
I am a midfielder attacking and shooting at the goal
And always waiting for a good opportunity.
I am a fancy red Ferrari sports car competing in the Grand Prix.
Always racing fairly.
I am a bright red apple shining with colour and sweetness
With plenty of tangy taste.
I am a golden three-seater sofa, soft and comfortable,
and delicate.
I am a wooden Irish traditional flute blowing like a
beautiful song of a bird.
I am a warm summer's day in the month of July.

Conall Mulhern (10)
St Colman's Primary School, Lambeg

Myself

I am a flowery meadow, with the flowers swaying
in the breeze,
I am a cheerful yellow, happy and energetic,
like the sun,
I am a juicy pear, sweet and soft,
I am a cat lazing in the sun, lying around
doing absolutely nothing,
I am a red rosebud swaying in the breeze,
I am a soft armchair comfy and warm to sit on,
I am Sidney, full of joy and happiness,
lighting up at parades,
I am satin, smooth, soft and silky,
I am a flute, light and airy.

Alice Hamill (10)
St Colman's Primary School, Lambeg

Myself

I am a plump little fruit on a tree
A juicy little pear on a branch
I am a cheetah running fast
To catch my prey like deer
I am a Viking, a drunk Viking,
Full of love and joy,
I am the president, making war
Between the nations,
I am a Gaelic footballer,
My team came first in the hurling
And won medals, cups and are in division two.

Aaron Feeney (10)
St Colman's Primary School, Lambeg

ME

I am rocky mountains with snowtops.
I am a tiny flower with white pebbles.
I am a juicy red apple.
I am a black cat so lucky.
I am a puppy so cute.
I am winter so breathtaking.
I am the sun rising in the morning.
I am an angel in the clouds.
I am the sign of frost.
I am a rose so tempting.
I am a newborn baby.
I am a bear so soft.
I am a tiger so brave and strong.
I am a lion so strong and brave.
I am a new-born baby so cute.
I am an axe as sharp as a razor.
I am bright in the light.
I am a tiger so fierce, strong and brave.

Melissa Marlow (10)
St Colman's Primary School, Lambeg

METAPHOR

I am a calm sea moving swiftly and gently waiting
peacefully until the boats come by
I am a daffodil blooming with its bright yellow warmth
Swaying from side to side giving off my lovely fragrance
I am a thrush with its soft, soothing melody singing in the morning
I am pink with happiness and enjoyment loving and caring for everyone
I am a red apple with its sweet juicy flavour
I am spring with silence of fresh growing grass and blooming flowers.

Maeve Power (10)
St Colman's Primary School, Lambeg

MYSELF!

I am a plant which is hot and bright,
Teaming in the sun in bright weather,
I am a golden star high above the trees,
Shining in the dark to make it bright,
I am a peach with skin so soft,
It's sweet and tastes lovely,
I am a cheetah that runs like the wind,
I am brown and black so fast as the wind,
I am a swimming kingfisher, so strong,
I swim so fast I'll win a race,
I am a golden tin whistle all short and nice,
Play so sweet and short, everyone listen to me,
I am a rocking chair moving very fast,
Rocking in my rocking chair and singing songs,
I am a month with bright colours,
I am blue and pink in this month,
I am a soft toy, small and cute,
I am small and lovely, soft and cute.

Emer O'Kane (10)
St Colman's Primary School, Lambeg

THE HEDGEHOG

Softly, softly
Hedgehog creeps
Slowly
Down the narrow street.

The moon is awake
The sun sleeps
And so must you
For it's half-past eight.

Katie Stanley (9)
St Colman's Primary School, Lambeg

SHE IS THE NORTH WIND BLOWING

She is the north wind blowing,
blowing through the trees.
She is the early morning,
the early morning breeze.
She is a rare stamp,
a stamp from Pakistan,
or a tasty sausage,
a sausage in a pan -
She is a crocodile
with a long and toothy grin.
She is a gleaming table,
varnished with polish from a tin.
She is a ball rolling,
rolling down the bowling alley.
She's a purple iris
in the garden -
or a tasty ice lolly.

Dillon McDonnell (10)
St Colman's Primary School, Lambeg

WHAT IS YOUR APPENDIX FOR?

What is your appendix for?
It's troubled me for a year or more,
I think it's like a piece of string
And the colour of the floor.

It's bothered me for years on end,
It's really driving me round the bend.
So should any of you ever find out
Remember to come and give me a shout!

Aidan Kelly (10)
St Colman's Primary School, Lambeg

ME: INSIDE MY HEAD

I am a cream fat tabby cat lazy and playful,
I am a summer's breeze warm and comforting,
I am a round orange soft and juicy,
I am a yellow daffodil waving in the wind,
I am a soft warm bed giving you comfort,
I am green bright, happy and cheerful
I am a drum beating fast and wildly
I am Florida energetic and fun
I am a meadow on a spring day
I am a river cool and refreshing
I am a roller-coaster exciting and scary
I am a puppy kind and happy
I am yellow bright and fun
I am a lion lazy and wild.

Kerry Watterson (9)
St Colman's Primary School, Lambeg

ME

I am a plum soft and sweet,
Pink inside, purple outside
I am a cute soft furry monkey
Always up to adventurous things
I am summer warm and full of goodness
Giving light and happiness to the world
I am yellow lovely and bright like the sun
Making love and light to the country
I am a plane very fast and smooth
Gliding through the air
I am a Shetland pony small and strong
Able to carry people on my back.

Roisin Maguire (10)
St Colman's Primary School, Lambeg

IMAGES OF ME

I am sometimes an excited playground
Waiting for my friends to come,
Listening carefully to the cheerful sounds
Of children playing monstrously,
I am the last rose falling apart every second,
Everyone admiring my red, pretty petals
Blowing in the wind,
I am a caring, soothing peach
Spreading flavour throughout the world,
Anyone who eats me shall bring peace to the world,
I am a brown, furry grizzly bear
Ready to rip off your head if you mistreat me,
If you are generous I will treat you with respect,
I am a spring baby ready to give out happiness
To all living things I meet.

Orlaith Moran (10)
St Colman's Primary School, Lambeg

ME MY NAME I CALL MYSELF

I am bright yellow like the warmth of the burning hot sun
And the beautiful yellow daffodils
And I am an enormous cello barking like a large, fierce, hungry dog.
I am the summer with a gentle breeze
And a wild chirping bird in the dark brown trees
Waiting for my young chicks to hatch.
I am a banana soft and squashy like a teddy bear
And a soft cushion snug and warm when people sit on me.

Meabh Trainor (10)
St Colman's Primary School, Lambeg

THE DIGESTIVE SYSTEM

My mouth is munching mangoes
My tongue is holding the taste,
When I swallow them and my rectum opens
Out will gush the waste.

But first they must travel through the oesophagus,
And down into my tummy,
There they will be swirled around
To make them very mushy.

Then they'll leave my stomach
And pass through my liver
I can't believe how food is digested,
It makes me shiver.

Now they will travel past the pancreas
That helps to soften foods
By using special juices
Which I think are rather good.

They are now in the small intestine
A large and twisting slide,
Now they've reached the large intestine
That is small and wide.

Hanging from the bottom of it,
Is the appendix which does nothing,
The food has reached journey's end
It took so long, it's shocking!

Emma McCrory (10)
St Colman's Primary School, Lambeg

MY DIGESTIVE SYSTEM

Chewing my dinner
Swallowing it down
Heading through my oesophagus
Churning round and round

Drinking lots of water
To help it flow
Moving quickly down the tube
It must go!

Now it's in the stomach
There we must part
Separate ways we must go
It's really an art

My bladder's full
My belly aches
My liver and onions
Are not for the take!

Large intestine
Small intestine
Wherever next?
The rectum the rectum
I've got to go quick

Can't get the light on
Oh dear what a mess!
What happens next?
You'll have to guess!

Lauren Bailie (10)
St Colman's Primary School, Lambeg

LISTEN

Listen to the sound
The loud loud sound
Of the wheels going
Round and round,
Listen to the sound
Big, big sound
Of the waves go slosh,
Listen to the whispers
Listen to the waves
Listen to everybody
That you meet
Listen to the teacher
As he tells you
Your homework,
Listen to the sounds
That nature makes,
Listen to the big
Bang bang
The bang of the
Door.

Conor Maguire (10)
St Colman's Primary School, Lambeg

CELEBRATION 2000

The year two thousand is coming soon.
Party poppers, hats and balloons
Will be everywhere.

There will be people in and
Out about pubs and clubs.
When the clock goes tick-tock
Everyone will shout 12 o'clock.

Restaurants, pubs and clubs
Will cost a big bill,
Lots of money going into the till.
You would need a big feed
For the money they charge and
Eat it with some speed.

Jamie Cassidy (9)
St Patrick's Primary School, Portrush

THE MILLENNIUM

Can I go to Lapland and play in a rock band,
instead of playing in the sand.

Will I go on holiday and ski in the bay,
and have a good day.

Will I sit in a fight and give everyone a fright.
Can I learn to drive and be so alive.

Can I have a PlayStation and build an army station,
Or say a joke, enjoy myself and drink some coke.

Conard McCullagh (9)
St Patrick's Primary School, Portrush

A Matter Of Seconds

Five seconds to go?
Five ticks of the clock.
Oh hurry, I say
Very impatiently.
We're ready to celebrate.
Am I dreaming?
Four ticks to go.
Why is the clock so slow?
The biggest parade has stopped.
Drums are beating.
Three ticks of the clock.
Big Ben will not stop.
Two seconds to go.
We're watching the Kelly show.
It's here! It's finally here!
We're in a new year.
Some people don't care about the year 2000
They say it's just another day,
Another boring old year.
But we go without fear into the year 2000.

Cal Hunter (8)
St Patrick's Primary School, Portrush

Five Seconds To Go

Five seconds to go
Oh I just can't believe it
I have to stay here and see
In the New Year.

Is my clock broken
Or is it just me.
Is it four seconds to go
Or is it just three.

All my family stand next to me.
We count 5, 4, 3, 2, 1.
Then we shout Happy New Year.

Then we have a party to celebrate.
So it's here and we jump around
With happiness and cheer.

Sorcha Loughrey (9)
St Patrick's Primary School, Portrush

CELEBRATION 2000

Here comes the year 2000
with party poppers and drink
then fireworks banging all night
with flashing lights from discos

People drinking beer and wine
everything going along as you planned it
a couple more minutes to the year 2000
waiting anxiously till the new century begins.

So the Millennium Dome is going to be complete
It was a long and difficult task
Now it is finished at last so be happy, have fun, be wild
Be just like a happy child.

So make your year be a good one
Make sure you have some fun!

Joanne Quinn (11)
St Patrick's Primary School, Portrush

THE YEAR 2000

We have waited for years and years and now it's nearly here.
They say it is going to be a special one and hopefully it will be full of fun.

But some of us fear as the Millennium Bug draws near,
Although there will be many a tear,
For no one knows what will disappear
And not everyone will be drinking beer.

So as the millennium flies near more of digital comes into gear.
Not only cars, TVs as well as many a toy and computers as well.
As the countdown comes to a close,
The people outside shout who knows?
They dance, they sing and they count,
We start from here 5, 4, 3, 2, 1

Now it has arrived . . . *Happy New Year!*

Kieran McNicholl (9)
St Patrick's Primary School, Portrush

CELEBRATION 2000

The year 2000 is near.
Everyone will be partying
and the men will be drinking beer.

The laser lights will be there
and the girls won't know what to wear
but when they get dressed
the men will be drunk
and they won't even notice they're there.

The Millennium Dome is being built
and thousands of restaurants are being filled;
with thousands of pounds being spend on food.
It will go well please, touch wood!

With fireworks and bangers and party poppers too,
it will be funny when my dad gets drunk
and wants to dance with you.

Ciara Etherson (11)
St Patrick's Primary School, Portrush

CELEBRATION 2000

I can't wait for the year 2000
It is the millennium
It is Jesus Christ's 2000th birthday.

I hope that I will be invited
To a party with my friends
Or go to the Millennium Dome.

Oh I can't wait for the year two thousand.
I will go to a fireworks display.

With bangers and sparklers
Rockets and Roman candles
Oh I can't wait.

The millennium is the best
But a century is OK
But a millennium is the best.

Fergus McFaul (11)
St Patrick's Primary School, Portrush

THE BIG DAY

Five minutes to go before
the millennium is here.
Maybe when I'm ten years old I will be
able to jump off the pier?

Will the Millennium Bug affect me?
I hope not.
It came to four minutes. I'll have a cup of tea.

Will there be hover boards in the millennium?
I hope so.

Three minutes to go, the millennium is near.
'Ten seconds to go,' Gerry Kelly said.

I shouted, '10, 9, 8, 7, 6, 5, 4, 3, 2, 1,
the millennium is here
Happy New Year.'

David Donaghy (8)
St Patrick's Primary School, Portrush

CELEBRATION 2000!

It's near the year 2000.
Let's all plan a party.
There'll be food, drinks and sweets
We'll dance to the music and listen to the drum beats.

We'll have good fun it'll be some crack
We'll have some fireworks and a little snack,
We'll eat lollies and lots of ice-cream,
We'll have so much fun it'll be like a dream.

There'll be balloons, bangers and candy sticks
And even top magic tricks,
There'll be music, dance and fun,
I'll eat loads of crisps and a very sticky bun.

When the clock strikes twelve everyone shouts 'Hooray!'
And that's the beginning of the year 2000's first day.

Roisin Donnelly (9)
St Patrick's Primary School, Portrush

FIVE MINUTES TO GO

It's the night before the 2000
Five minutes to go,
I feel that I'm all tangled up.

Four minutes to go
I'm staring at the clock
Listening to the tick-tock.

Three minutes to go
I just can't wait.
This year I will be a big ten.
A double celebration in the millennium.

Two minutes to go,
Jerry Kelly said 'My throat is dry
I need a drink. All the excitement is
Going round in my head.'

One minute to go the clock strikes twelve
I give a big cheer
Happy New Year.

Meghan Doole (8)
St Patrick's Primary School, Portrush

FIVE SECONDS TO GO

Five seconds to go
I just can't believe it
Is my clock broken?

Four seconds to go
I can't wait for this big big day
The millennium is on its way.

Three seconds to go
I just can't wait
I am shouting go, go, go, just go.

Two seconds to go
I am so excited
I can't wait,
I am so delighted.

One second to go
What shall I do?
Will I go over to my mum
I'll go outside and play on my bike

At last the year 2000 is here
We shout with happiness and joy
Happy New Year.

Dean Murphy (9)
St Patrick's Primary School, Portrush

2000

Oh is my clock broken we are all woken
by the sound of glee it's all happening to me.
It's excitement all around and there's
Cake on the ground.

The bar men are drinking their beer with no fear.
There's too much excitement in my head
And I think I'm nearly dead
And Mrs Bo Peep is calling for her sheep.

Adrian McCullagh (9)
St Patrick's Primary School, Portrush

CELEBRATION 2000

We are going to have a party
We will play lots of games
With food and drink and laughter
To celebrate the year

We will turn off all the lights
A couple of minutes before
So when the clock hits midnight
The year 2000 is here

We will sing and talk
Shout and clap
Because the year 2000 has come
We can all jump up and down

Now we can start the party
And pop the party poppers
Remember it is Jesus' birthday
So I say a little prayer

When the party is over
We all tidy up
We will go to bed
And say goodnight.

Owen McLaughlin (9)
St Patrick's Primary School, Portrush

COUNTING TO 2000

Five seconds to go I'm so excited
Everyone is really delighted
Standing waiting watching the clock
I wish it would tick-tock

Four seconds to go I'm full of joy
the room is filled with girls and boys
Everyone dancing, everyone gay
Everyone waiting for this big day.

Three seconds to go tension mounting
Everyone starts counting
Wishing the time would go quickly
Oh I'm starting to feel sickly.

Two seconds to go, getting ready
Adults sway unsteady
Bells start chiming for the countdown
Uncle Denis has to sit down.

One second to go, countdown starts
10 9 8 7 6 5 4 3 2 1
Everyone singing *Auld Lang Syne*
In a circle holding hands

Waiting is over it has come
Happy 2000 everyone.

Lauren Doherty (8)
St Patrick's Primary School, Portrush

CELEBRATION 2000!

'Can we have a party?'
said I to my mum.
'Not this year but
the year 2001.'

'But Mum you promised.'
'Did I?'
'Yes.'
'Well I'm sorry but the answer is no.'
So I said 'OK,' with a great big sigh.

And I lay in bed till
morning was nigh . . .
That night my mum went out.
So I said, 'Goodbye . . .'

I'm going to have a party,
one of my very own
and no one shall stop me
and I won't be alone . . .

I'll invite all my friends
but I'm not too good at being a host . . .
I won't invite Sarah
because she likes to boast.

'This party's the best,'
said Jessica to me.
Then in comes my mother,
'Would you like some tea?'

What! Well, she's completely mad . . .
I know I'll just call Dad!

Amy Lagan (9)
St Patrick's Primary School, Portrush

CELEBRATION 2000!

We're going to be partying
on the year 2000AD with crisps,
drinks and beer, and we'll stay
up to midnight to help bring in
the *new year!*

With cakes and cheese,
and not forgetting crackers.
Then with music, buns and
games we'll all have lots of fun.

With bangers and party poppers,
laughter song and dance.
When the clock strikes twelve
The wine glasses will go up
And everyone will cheer 'Happy New Year.'

Then we will party a little while more,
But then we will go to bed
And snore and snore and snore.
ZZZzzzzz.

Gemma Hegarty (9)
St Patrick's Primary School, Portrush

CELEBRATION 2000

A great party about to start,
Ice-cream and apple tart.
All for the 2000th year,
No one with a single tear.

Building a great Dome,
It will be *fun's* first home!
People being good,
Like they always should.

What shall I do
When New Year's Eve is through?
The parties will be done,
And so will vanish all the fun.

Claire McNally (9)
St Patrick's Primary School, Portrush

WAITING FOR THE YEAR 2000

I'm waiting for the year 2000.
What's going to happen to me?
What will I do in my spare time?
Will the Millennium Bug affect me?

Will I be able to watch TV
Or play on the computer,
When I have finished my tea?
Will the Millennium Bug affect me?

Will I be able to defrost the bread,
Or will the microwave be nearly dead?
Will I be able to listen to my CD?
Will the Millennium Bug affect me?

Will I still be the same?
I'm not a computer, microwave or TV.
I am a girl of eight year old,
So will the Millennium Bug affect me?

Niamh Quinn (8)
St Patrick's Primary School, Portrush

CELEBRATION 2000

We're going to have a party and a fantastic celebration.
There's going to be some crackers, food, fun and games.
We'll also celebrate our Saviour Jesus Christ, for he is 2000 years.
We'll celebrate all night with the world and God's creation.

This night will go on forever.
It will be a brilliant night.
There will be fireworks, laser lights and dancing.
This night will be fantastic for me and hopefully everyone.

This year will be very special.
There will be a Millennium Dome.
Not everyone likes this thing
Because it cost 70 million pounds.

Martin McAlister (10)
St Patrick's Primary School, Portrush

A NEW YEAR

Five seconds to go I just can't wait.
We're all getting ready to celebrate.
Mum pours the coke, and I ask, 'Is that mine?'
As we get ready to say goodbye to '99.

The race is on for the new year on the Kelly Show.
This is what I hear. Four seconds to go, no wait it's three.
We all get together, Mum, Dad and me.

Two seconds to go, I jump up and cheer
All my family are standing near.
One second to go. No it's here!
Hip-hip-hooray for the New Year.

Mary McCrory (8)
St Patrick's Primary School, Portrush

THE RAT TRAP

The deadly trap,
looming in the bushes,
cold, harsh metal
luring animals into its jaws.
The heart-wrenching scream
of rats and rabbits
caught in its teeth
after sniffing out the food.

Its bloodstained teeth
are like a lion's after a kill.
It's awful to think
of the amount of lives cut short.
How many more squeals
out of that trap will I hear?
How many more lives will go?

Laura Cunningham (11)
Springfarm Primary School

CELEBRATION 2000

It could be a disaster,
it could be great fun,
but whatever happens it will be the millennium.
The parties, the fun for everyone.
The work, the play and the great day,
will it be sad or will it be bad.
It feels fun for everyone.

Martin Davey (9)
Straid Primary School

CELEBRATION 2000

When the year 2000 comes
It will bring the biggest party.
Everybody will be counting down
10 to 0.

There'll be
fireworks to light up the sky
and everyone will be wearing
nice clothes, when they are celebrating.

But there are some bad things too.
Computers might shut down.
Hospital equipment might not work
but that's not what we're celebrating.

We're celebrating the millennium.

Edmund Davis (11)
Straid Primary School

CELEBRATION 2000

2000 the year,
So everyone cheer.
The Millennium Dome
And people leaving home.

We will hear a band,
And lend a hand.
There'll be drinks and food.
Adults remembering their childhood.

Mums and dads giving a hug,
But what about the Millennium Bug!
Parties being hosted.
Invitations have been posted.

Everyone saying 10, 9, 8 . . .
Everyone with a date.
Now it is gone
We will look forward to the next dawn.

Christopher Walker (10)
Straid Primary School

CELEBRATION 2000!

Big Ben is ticking
all the time.
Until it reaches midnight
on the 31st December.
It's coming near
at the end of the year.
We are all very lucky to
hopefully be around.
Parties, dances
food and drink.
Wondrous places
to be seen.
Famous people
on the scene.
But until that time
has been and gone
we can only prepare
and dream.

Jane McAllister (10)
Straid Primary School

CELEBRATION 2000

The millennium is nearly here,
It's the beginning of a new year.
It may be time to laugh and shout,
But the computer bug is going about!

There's noise and fun and parties galore,
You wish there could be a lot, lot more.
That's not what all the millennium is about,
You haven't forgot about the Millennium Dome no doubt!

I hope everyone enjoys the new year,
With a good laugh and a very good cheer!

Celebrate good times
Come on!
Join the millennium!

Ariane Moore (11)
Straid Primary School

CELEBRATION 2000

C elebrations for the year 2000.
E veryone enjoying themselves.
L ots of people out for fun.
E veryone having a good time.
B right lights everywhere.
R ushing people getting everything done before the new year.
A ll year long they've been preparing for the new year.
T housands of people on the streets.
I ndoor and outdoor parties going on.
O pen invitations to come to all the fun.
N ew year new hope for everyone.

Craig Bunting (9)
Straid Primary School

CELEBRATION 2000

C lowns for a party and some party hats.
E lephants go down the street in the carnival.
L ollies you lick which are in party bags.
E ggs you eat that are made from chocolate and treats.
B is for buns you love to gobble up.
R is for riding the horses that you ride.
A is for apple the fruit that you eat.
T is for tigers and all of the animals in the parades.
I is for I love to celebrate.
O is for orchestras that are playing some songs.
N is for noisy and the sound of everyone

2000 is the year it will all happen!

Joel Dundee (9)
Straid Primary School

CELEBRATION 2000

It is 12.00pm at night,
and everyone's up.
Up to see the millennium.
People are dancing,
dancing all night
and now there is laughter,
laughter alright.

Shouting and cheering and chattering,
and parties going all night.
Fireworks go *bang, bang!*
They give me a scary fright.
Now it's time to say goodnight.

Sarah Harrison (9)
Straid Primary School

CELEBRATION 2000!

M is for the magic shows that perform
　　is for the music that plays on the stage.

I is for the impressive fireworks.
　　is for the incredible atmosphere.

L is for the laughter from people
　　is for the limousine that will bring the stars.

L is for the list of things in the Dome
　　is for the looking of the people at the Dome.

E is for exciting things in the Dome
　　is for the enjoyment that people will have.

N is for the noise that is heard
　　is for New Year's Day.

N is for the next millennium
　　is for new inventions to look forward to.

I is for the inside of the Dome
　　is for the interesting things in the Dome.

U is for uncertain events which might happen
　　is for the unique Dome.

M is for the marvellous Dome
　　is for the magnificent crowd.

James Hutchinson (9)
Straid Primary School

CELEBRATION 2000

It's coming up to twelve o'clock
It's near the millennium.
People sing and people shout,
People are laughing, people are giggling.

Family and friends,
Food and drink,
Fun and fantasy.
It's nearly the millennium!

Hannah Buckley (9)
Straid Primary School

CELEBRATION 2000

Fireworks go *bang, bang*
Street lights switch on.
Here comes the millennium, 10, 9, 8 . . .

People chitter, chatter all night long.
Dogs barking
Cats purring.
Here comes the millennium, 10, 9 8 . . .

People jump for joy
Parties start *hooray!*
Here comes the millennium, 10, 9, 8 . . .

All the world will be awake that night
While people watch the firework displays
Here comes the millennium, 10, 9, 8 . . .

London has built a Dome
It's big and strong and holds our history.
Here comes the millennium, 10, 9, 8 . . .

It's 12pm at night
It's the night of the millennium
The sky is sparking silver, blue and pink
And now it's over for another thousand years.

Glenn Irwin (9)
Straid Primary School

CELEBRATION 2000!

People cheer
they're glad to hear
the millennium is on its way.

They're building a Dome
at Greenwich, time's home.
The millennium is here to stay.

So join in the celebration
or even take vacation.
The millennium is coming, get ready.

Will your computer explode
with the new year 2000, date code.
The millennium is coming, get ready,
get steady, 10, 9, 8, 7, 6, 5, 4, 3, 2, 1 . . .
. . .

The celebration has
started!

Louise Forsythe (11)
Straid Primary School

CELEBRATION 2000

There are lots of parties
And lots of things to do.
It is very magical
And it is cheerful too.

Lots of exciting things happen
And famous people come.
Now is the time for remembering,
When you and I were young.

We are lucky to see it,
Not very many do
And we should always thank the Lord
That we are going to.

Lauren Glasgow (9)
Straid Primary School

CELEBRATION 2000

Isn't it great to see the millennium come in.
With parties here and parties there and parties everywhere.
Hip-hip-hooray this is the day for the millennium is coming.

There's lots of things to do.
Hurry up. Hurry up.
We can't stop to chat.
Hip-hip-hooray this is the day to be getting ready for everything.

Parties everywhere there's lots of things to do
Art, exhibitions and fireworks.
Hip-hip-hooray this is the day for the millennium is coming.

Munching and crunching fabulous food.
People spending lots of money on it.
It's coming soon, hip-hip-hooray this is the day.

Samuel Forsythe (8)
Straid Primary School